Math Games

180 Reproducible Activities to
Motivate, Excite, and Challenge Students
Grades 6–12

Judith A. Muschla
and
Gary Robert Muschla

JOSSEY-BASS
A Wiley Imprint
www.josseybass.com

Published by Jossey-Bass
A Wiley Imprint
989 Market Street, San Francisco, CA 94103-1741   www.josseybass.com

Jossey-Bass books and products are available through most bookstores. To contact Jossey-Bass directly call our Customer Care Department within the U.S. at 800-956-7739, outside the U.S. at 317-572-3986, or fax 317-572-4002.

Jossey-Bass also publishes its books in a variety of electronic formats. Some content that appears in print may not be available in electronic books.

ISBN 0-7879-7081-6

Printed in the United States of America
FIRST EDITION
PB Printing   10 9 8

For Erin

About the Authors

Judith A. Muschla received her B.A. in mathematics from Douglass College at Rutgers University and is certified to teach K–12. She has taught mathematics in South River, New Jersey, for more than twenty-five years. She has taught math at various levels at South River High School, ranging from basic skills through calculus. She has also taught at South River Middle School, where, in her capacity as a team leader, she helped revise the mathematics curriculum to reflect the Standards of the National Council of Teachers of Mathematics, coordinated interdisciplinary units, and conducted mathematics workshops for teachers and parents. She was a recipient of the 1990–91 Governor's Teacher Recognition Program Award in New Jersey, and she was named the 2002 South River Public School District Teacher of the Year. Along with teaching, she has been a member of the state Standards Review Panel for the Mathematics Core Curriculum Contents Standards in New Jersey.

Math Games is the seventh book Gary and Judith Muschla have co-authored. They have also written *The Math Teacher's Book of Lists* (1995); *Hands-on Math Projects with Real-Life Applications* (1996); *Math Starters! 5- to 10-Minute Activities to Make Kids Think, Grades 6–12* (1999); *The Geometry Teacher's Activities Kit* (2000); *Math Smart! Over 220 Ready-to-Use Activities to Motivate and Challenge Students, Grades 6–12* (2002); and *The Algebra Teacher's Activities Kit* (2003), all published by Jossey-Bass.

Gary Robert Muschla received his B.A. and M.A.T. from Trenton State College and taught at Appleby School in Spotswood, New Jersey, for more than twenty-five years. He spent many of his years in the classroom teaching mathematics at the elementary level. He has also taught reading and writing and is a successful author. He is a member of the Authors Guild and the National Writers Association.

He has written several resources for teachers, among them *The Writing Teacher's Book of Lists* (1991, second edition 2003); *Writing Workshop Survival Kit* (1993); *English Teacher's Great Books Activities Kit* (1994); *Reading Workshop Survival Kit* (1997); *Ready-to-Use Reading Proficiency Lessons and Activities, 4th Grade Level* (2002); *Ready-to-Use Reading Proficiency Lessons and Activities, 8th Grade Level* (2002); and *Ready-to-Use Reading Proficiency Lessons and Activities, 10th Grade Level* (2003), all published by Jossey-Bass. He currently writes and serves as a consultant in education.

Acknowledgments

We would like to thank Michael Pfister, assistant superintendent, South River (New Jersey) Public Schools; Paul Coleman, principal of South River High School; and our colleagues for their support of our efforts in writing this book.

We also thank Steve D. Thompson, Ph.D., our editor, for his support of this project.

Thanks also to our daughter, Erin, the first reader of the manuscript, for finding our many oversights and omissions in the early drafts.

We appreciate the efforts of Michele Julien, our production editor, in guiding the manuscript through the production process; and we would like to thank Diane Turso for her proofreading.

Finally, we would like to thank our students, who have made teaching a challenging, exciting, and rewarding experience for us.

Introduction

To meet the demands of mathematics instruction today, math teachers must provide their students with materials that reflect the Principles and Standards of the National Council of Teachers of Mathematics. While making sure their students master the basics, they must emphasize critical thinking, problem-solving skills, and the use of technology. All are essential to prepare students for their future.

The most successful math teachers, however, go beyond all this. They offer materials and activities that are both stimulating and challenging, that help students not only master mathematic principles and concepts but appreciate and enjoy math as well.

This is the purpose of *Math Games*. Although the activities are designed to be playful, fun, and freewheeling, they are founded on specific mathematical skills based on the Standards of the NCTM for grades six through twelve. Because many of the activities are somewhat unconventional, they require students to think critically and "outside the box" and rely on sound mathematical sense.

We trust that *Math Games* will enhance your instruction and help your students better understand, appreciate, and enjoy math.

How to Use This Resource

This resource is divided into seven sections, containing a total of 180 activities. An Answer Key is included at the end of the book. Following is a brief description of each section.

Section One, "Whole Numbers," has twenty-three activities. This section includes a variety of activities involving basic operations, rounding, factors, multiples, powers, order of operations, and patterns.

Section Two, "Fractions, Decimals, and Percents," contains thirty activities. This section covers such topics as equivalent fractions, sequence, factors, lowest common denominators, operations with fractions and decimals, place value, rounding, scientific notation, ratios, proportions, and operations with percents.

Section Three, "Geometry," has twenty-six activities. Topics include angles, lines, polygons, triangles, quadrilaterals, congruent and similar figures, right triangles, the Pythagorean Theorem, symmetry, circles, three-dimensional figures, and Euler's Formula.

Section Four, "Measurement," contains thirty activities. The activities include customary and metric units of length, liquid, and weight; time; temperature; measurement of angles; perimeter and area of quadrilaterals and triangles; area and circumference of circles; volume; and surface area.

Section Five, "Algebra," has thirty-five activities. The activities cover topics such as expressions, number lines, operations with integers, functions, equations, the coordinate plane, quadratic equations, and inequalities.

Section Six, "Data Analysis," contains nine activities. The activities of this section include mean, median, and mode; graphs; matrices; data displays; and probability and odds.

Section Seven, "Potpourri," contains twenty-seven activities that cover a variety of skills and topics. This section includes activities on basic operations; Roman numerals; word problems; patterns; equations; rotations, translations, and reflections; and mathematics vocabulary.

Each activity stands alone and is numbered according to its section. For example, Activity 1–8, "Who Am I?" (Factors, Primes, and Composites), is the eighth activity of Section One. Each activity is titled and also labeled with the topic or skill it addresses. This label appears on the top of each worksheet and with the title in the Table of Contents, making it easy for you to match activities with the needs of your students and the requirements of your instructional program. For example, if you wish to supplement a review lesson on operations with fractions, you might consider Activity 2–7, "Think About This" (All Operations with Fractions).

The activities may be used for various purposes: to supplement your math program, for reinforcement, for challenges, or for substitute plans. Moreover, the activities are designed for simple implementation. Each has easy-to-follow directions for the students, and most require no materials other than the reproducible.

The activities in each section follow the sequence of a typical math curriculum and generally progress from basic to challenging. Many involve multiple skills—and just plain old math sense. You should select those activities that best satisfy the needs and abilities of your students.

The Answer Key at the end of the book is organized according to section. Most problems have one answer. For those that have several possible answers, examples of possible answers are provided.

The activities of *Math Games* serve a variety of purposes. We recommend that you choose the activities that complement your instruction and meet the needs of your students.

Judy and Gary Muschla

Contents

About the Authors   iv

Acknowledgments   v

Introduction   vi

Section 1: Whole Numbers   1

1–1. **There's a Place for Everything**   2
Operations and Place Value

1–2. **Finding Missing Numbers**   3
Operations with Whole Numbers

1–3. **Finding the Largest and Smallest**   4
Operations with Whole Numbers

1–4. **A Number Chain**   5
Operations with Whole Numbers

1–5. **Which Is Greater?**   6
Operations and Rounding with Whole Numbers

1–6. **The Trio Rounds to . . .**   7
Rounding Numbers

1–7. **A Fact About You**   8
Factors and Perfect Squares

1–8. **Who Am I?**   9
Factors, Primes, and Composites

1–9. **Which One Does Not Belong?**   10
Attributes of Numbers

1–10. **Cross Number Puzzle: Whole Numbers**   11
Number Puzzle

1–11. **The Powers of Primes**   12
Exponents

1–12. **Cubes and Squares**   13
Exponents

1–13. **An Exponential Typo**   14
Exponents

1–14. **Euclid and the GCF**   15
Greatest Common Factor

1–15. **Finding the LCM Using the GCF**   16
Least Common Multiple

1–16. **The Missing Symbols**   17
Order of Operations

1–17. **What a Mix-Up!**   18
Order of Operations

1–18. **A Perfect 10**   19
Order of Operations

1–19. **Not-So-Famous Firsts for Presidents**   20
Order of Operations

1–20. **What's Next?**   21
Patterns

1–21. **Numbers of All Kinds**   22
Types of Numbers

1–22. **Val's Baby-Sitting Job**   23
Application of Numbers

1–23. **Is the Price Right?**   24
Number Sense

Section 2: Fractions, Decimals, and Percents   25

2–1. **Fractional Trivia**   26
Equivalent Fractions

2–2. **Odd Fraction Out**   27
Equivalent Fractions

2–3. **Don't Be Redundant**   28
Fraction and Decimal Equivalences

2–4. **Out of Order**   29
Fraction Sequence

2–5. **Don't Be Square**   30
Greatest Common Factor and Lowest Common Denominator

2–6. **Boxes and Numbers**   31
All Operations with Proper Fractions

2–7. **Think About This**   32
All Operations with Fractions

2–8. **Filling in Fractions**   33
All Operations with Mixed Fractions

2–9. **Making a Match**   34
All Operations with Mixed Numbers

2–10. **Not Really Complex at All**   35
Complex Fractions

2–11. **Making a Point**   36
Place Value

2–12. **More or Less**   37
Comparing Decimals

2–13. **What Comes First?**   38
Decimal Order

2–14. **What's the Point?**   39
Decimals and Equivalent Fractions

2–15. **Decimal Round-up** 40
Rounding Decimals

2–16. **A Decimal Cross Number Puzzle** 41
All Operations with Decimals

2–17. **The Missing Link** 42
All Operations with Decimals

2–18. **Get the Point** 43
All Operations with Decimals

2–19. **At the Mall** 44
All Operations with Money

2–20. **Do You Have Some Change?** 45
Money and Change

2–21. **Human Body Statistics** 46
Scientific Notation

2–22. **Celestial Facts** 47
Standard Form

2–23. **Right and Wrong** 48
All Operations with Fractions and Decimals

2–24. **Mystery Ratios** 49
Ratios

2–25. **How Do You Rate?** 50
Ratios

2–26. **What's Cooking?** 51
Proportions

2–27. **Finding the Third** 52
Fraction, Decimal, and Percent Equivalences

2–28. **Times Change** 53
Three Types of Percent Problems

2–29. **Percents with a Twist** 54
Three Types of Percent Problems

2–30. **Short Work of Percents** 55
Percents of Numbers and Percent of Increase

Section 3: Geometry 57

3–1. **What's the Angle?** 58
Angles and Angle Pairs

3–2. **Quilting Lines** 59
Parallel and Perpendicular Lines

3–3. **Counting Sides** 60
Polygons

3–4. **Sometimes It's Right!** 61
Acute, Obtuse, and Right Triangles

3–5. **Find the Right Word** 62
Types of Triangles

3–6. **What's My Line?** 63
Lines of a Triangle

3–7. **Angles and Measures** 64
Angles of Parallel Lines and Transversals

3–8. **A Quadrilateral by Any Other Name** 65
Types of Quadrilaterals

3–9. **What's the Measure?** 66
Angles of Quadrilaterals

3–10. **A Polygon Word Find** 67
Terms of Polygons and Angles

3–11. **Always, Sometimes, Never** 68
Angles and Polygons

3–12. **Different and Yet the Same** 69
Angles and Polygons

3–13. **What's the Relationship?** 71
Angles and Polygons

3–14. **All, Some, or No** 72
Congruent and Similar Figures

3–15. **Finding the Proof** 73
Congruent Triangles

3–16. **Finding Right Triangles** 74
Pythagorean Theorem

3–17. **Figure This** 75
Special Right Triangles

3–18. **Picture This** 76
Lines of Symmetry

3–19. **Spinning Around** 77
Line and Rotational Symmetry

3–20. **Don't Go in Circles!** 78
Terms of a Circle

3–21. **A Circle Word Find** 79
Circle Terms

3–22. **Complete the Circle** 80
Lines and Angles of a Circle

3–23. **A Circular Chain** 81
Lengths of Segments in Circles

3–24. **3-D Word Scramble** 82
Terms of Three-Dimensional Figures

3–25. **Finding 3-D Figures** 83
Three-Dimensional Figures

3–26. **A Great Swiss Mathematician** 84
Euler's Formula

Section 4: Measurement 85

4–1. **Going to Great Lengths** 86
Customary Units of Length

4–2. **The Long and Short of It** 87
Metric Units of Length

4–3. **Going the Distance** 88
Lengths of Segments

4–4. **Not Just for Cooking** 89
Customary Units of Liquid Measure

4–5. **Odd Measure Out** 90
Customary Units of Length, Liquid, and Weight

4–6. **Getting to the Basics** 91
SI Units

4–7. **Equal or Not Equal** 92
Metric Units of Length, Liquid, and Weight

4–8. **It's About Time** 93
Computation with Time

4–9. **Never Enough Time** 94
Computation with Time

4–10. **Timely Words** 95
Words Relating to Time

4–11. **Coded Equations** 96
Units of Measure

4–12. **How Do You Measure Up?** 97
Equivalent Measures

4–13. **Take Your Measure** 98
Miscellaneous Measures

4–14. **Matching Temperatures** 99
Fahrenheit and Celsius Scales

4–15. **A Matter of Degree** 100
Angle Measures

4–16. **A Slice of the Circle** 101
Angle Measures: Degrees and Radians

4–17. **Finding the Way Around** 102
Perimeters and Circumferences of Plane Figures

4–18. **Going Around in "Squares"** 103
Perimeters of Irregular Figures

4–19. **Sketching It Out** 104
Area and Perimeter of Squares and Rectangles

4–20. **Different Figures, Same Areas** 105
Areas of Plane Figures

4–21. **Drawing Geometric Figures** 106
Area and Perimeter of Plane Figures

4–22. **All Related**   107
Areas of Rhombi, Triangles, and Rectangles

4–23. **Going Full Circle**   108
Measurements of Circles

4–24. **Know What Formula to Use**   109
Perimeter, Circumference, and Area Formulas

4–25. **Formulas to the Max**   110
Advanced Area Formulas for Polygons

4–26. **A Step Beyond**   111
Areas of Volumes and Right Prisms

4–27. **Same and Different**   113
Volume and Surface Area

4–28. **What's the Value?**   115
Volume and Surface Area

4–29. **Double Trouble**   116
Various Measures of Length, Area, Volume, and Surface Area

4–30. **Measuring Up**   117
Customary Units of Measurement

Section 5: Algebra   **119**

5–1. **Finding Solutions**   120
Expressions

5–2. **According to the Facts**   121
Expressions

5–3. **A Sweet Time Line**   122
Number Line

5–4. **A Place for Everything**   123
Number Line

5–5. **Finding Equal Expressions**   124
Addition and Subtraction of Integers

5–6. **Counting Down**   125
Multiplication and Division of Integers

5–7. **Finding the Largest and Smallest**   126
All Operations with Integers

5–8. **Integer Facts**   127
All Operations with Integers

5–9. **Parentheses, Please**   128
Order of Operations

5–10. **Numbers in Boxes**   129
Operations with Real Numbers

5–11. **Putting the Fun in Functions**   130
Functions

5–12. **Finding the Fourth**   131
Functions

5–13. **Absolutely Sure!**   132
Absolute Value

5–14. **The Lucky 13**   133
Expressions

5–15. **An Equation Chain**   134
Equations

5–16. **Matching Equations**   135
Equations

5–17. **Not Quite Right**   136
Equations

5–18. **Correct Solutions**   137
Equations

5–19. **Get to the Point!**   138
Coordinate Plane

5–20. **Common Knowledge**   139
Coordinate Plane

5–21. **A Shining Star**   140
Systems of Equations

5–22. **Doubletalk**   141
Systems of Equations

5–23. **A Radical Change**   142
Radicals

5–24. **Radical Matches**   143
Basic Operations with Radicals

5–25. **All in the Range**   144
Quadratic Functions with Perfect Squares

5–26. **And the Answer Is . . .**   145
Quadratic Equations

5–27. **Varying Values**   146
Quadratic Equations

5–28. **Common to Both**   147
Common Factors of Polynomials

5–29. **Something's Wrong**   148
Linear Inequalities

5–30. **Absolutely Correct**   149
Absolute Value Equations and Inequalities

5–31. **Find the Functions**   150
Composite Functions

5–32. **Relativity**   151
Families of Functions

5–33. **Just Passing Through**   152
Graphs

5–34. **Defining Expressions**   153
       Domains of Functions

5–35. **How Well Do You Function?**   154
       Algebra of Functions

Section 6: Data Analysis   **155**

6–1.   **Passing the Test**   156
       Mean, Median, and Mode

6–2.   **Inserting the Missing Data**   157
       Mean, Median, and Mode

6–3.   **Charting the Temperatures**   158
       Line Graphs

6–4.   **A Piece of the Pie**   159
       Circle Graphs

6–5.   **Mark That Date**   160
       Simple Probability

6–6.   **All About Data**   161
       Data Displays

6–7.   **A Matrix Chain**   162
       Addition and Subtraction of Matrices

6–8.   **The Missing Elements**   163
       Matrix Multiplication

6–9.   **The Odds Are . . .**   164
       Probability and Odds

Section 7: Potpourri   **165**

7–1.   **Deuces Are Wild**   166
       Basic Operations

7–2.   **Finding Missing Numbers**   167
       Basic Operations

7–3.   **Make a Quiz**   168
       Basic Operations

7–4.   **Reading the Signs**   169
       Basic Operations

7–5.   **Wheeling Around**   170
       Basic Operations

7–6.   **Math Tic-Tac-Toe**   171
       Equivalent Expressions

7–7.   **It's a Date**   172
       Roman Numerals

7–8.   **Left to Right or Right to Left**   173
       Palindromes

7–9.   **What's the Problem?**   174
        Word Problems

7–10.   **And the Question Is . . .**   175
        Word Problems

7–11.   **You're the Teacher**   176
        Word Problems

7–12.   **Finding Missing Information**   177
        Word Problems

7–13.   **Create a Pattern**   178
        Patterns

7–14.   **Signs**   179
        Order of Operations

7–15.   **Numbers and Values**   180
        Equivalencies

7–16.   **A Mixed-up Magic Square**   181
        Computation

7–17.   **Math Word Chains**   182
        Mathematics Vocabulary

7–18.   **Finding the 10s**   183
        Variables and Expressions

7–19.   **Code Cracking**   184
        Equations

7–20.   **Turning It Around**   185
        Rotations, Translations, and Reflections

7–21.   **What's the Connection?**   186
        Numbers and Relationships

7–22.   **Tracing Networks**   187
        Networks

7–23.   **Very "Plane"**   188
        Vectors

7–24.   **The "Bases" of This Activity**   189
        Bases 2, 5, and 8

7–25.   **Sines, Cosines, and Tangents**   190
        Trigonometric Ratios

7–26.   **Cones, Cones, Cones**   191
        Conic Sections

7–27.   **Not Just for Techies**   192
        Computer and Internet Words

        Answer Key   193

Section 1

WHOLE NUMBERS

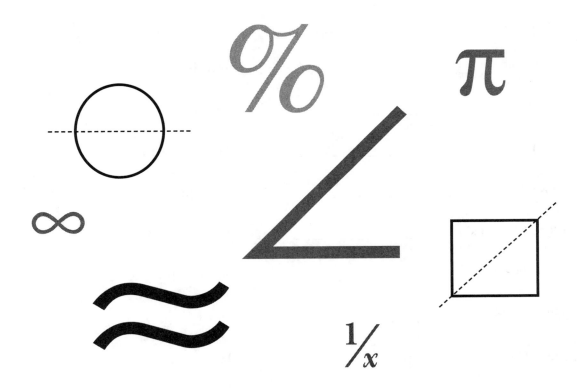

NAME _____ DATE _____

1-1 THERE'S A PLACE FOR EVERYTHING

Find each sum, difference, product, or quotient. Then circle the indicated place in your answer. The numbers you circle in your answers should be a digit from 0 to 9. Each odd digit should appear twice in the circled numbers, and each even digit should appear only once.

1. $345 + 296 =$ _____   Tens place

2. $531 - 456 =$ _____   Tens place

3. $326 \times 82 - 3{,}164 =$ _____   Thousands place

4. $801 \times 39 =$ _____   Hundreds place

5. $684 \div 36 =$ _____   Ones place

6. $3{,}015 - 498 =$ _____   Hundreds place

7. $4{,}079 \times 86 =$ _____   Tens place

8. $34 + 30 + 69 + 128 =$ _____   Tens place

9. $7{,}560 \div 35 \times 79 =$ _____   Thousands place

10. $305 \times 602 =$ _____   Ones place

11. $100 \times 74 \div 10 \times 427 =$ _____   Ten thousands place

12. $687 - 488 =$ _____   Hundreds place

13. $5{,}490 \div 305 =$ _____   Ones place

14. $148 \times 379 =$ _____   Ten thousands place

15. $32{,}886 \div 9 =$ _____   Thousands place

NAME _____ DATE _____

1-2 FINDING MISSING NUMBERS

Find the missing numbers so that each group of problems has the same answer.

Group 1

$$15 + \boxed{} = 52$$

$$74 - \boxed{} = 52$$

$$\boxed{} \times 2 = 52$$

$$\boxed{} \overline{)156} = 52$$

Group 2

$$\boxed{} + 98 = 315$$

$$\boxed{} - 607 = 315$$

$$15 \times \boxed{} = 315$$

$$2\overline{)\boxed{}} = 315$$

Group 3

$$738 + \boxed{} = 1{,}085$$

$$\boxed{} - 263 = 1{,}085$$

$$35 \times \boxed{} = 1{,}085$$

$$\boxed{} \overline{)5{,}425} = 1{,}085$$

NAME _____ DATE _____

1-3 FINDING THE LARGEST AND SMALLEST

Use the numbers below to fill in each box according to the directions given.

2   3   4   6   8   9

Find the largest odd sum.

1.

2.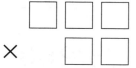

Find the smallest difference. It must be larger than zero.

3.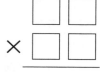

4.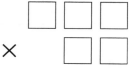

Find the largest product.

5.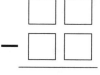

6.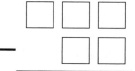

Find the smallest product.

7.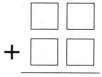

8.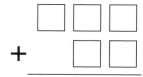

Find the smallest quotient. It must be a whole number with no remainder.

9.

Find the largest quotient. It must be a whole number with no remainder.

10.

NAME _____ DATE _____

1–4 A NUMBER CHAIN

Follow the directions of each number chain. Write your answers in the spaces provided.

1. Start with 26. Multiply by 13; add 222; divide by 16; multiply by 18; divide by 9; multiply

    by 56; subtract 392; divide by 126; subtract 2. _____

2. Start with 706. Subtract 398; add 25; divide by 111; multiply by 98; divide by 42; multiply

    by 128; divide by 56; multiply by 98; subtract 1,492. _____

3. Think of a three-digit number. Write it here. _____ Multiply it by 3; add 18; multi-

    ply by 4; subtract 6; divide by 6; multiply by 8; add 8; divide by 16; subtract 6. _____

    How does your answer compare to your original number? _____

    _____

4. Think of a four-digit number. Write it here. _____ Double the number; add 10;

    multiply by 12; divide by 8; multiply by 9; add 189; divide by 27; subtract 13. _____

    How does your answer compare to your original number? _____

    _____

NAME _____ DATE _____

1–5 WHICH IS GREATER?

Find all the sums, differences, products, or quotients for the problems in columns A and B. Write your answers in the spaces provided. Compare the answers in both columns for each problem, and circle the larger answer. Then follow the special directions for problems 11 through 13.

Column A   **Column B**

1. $85 \times 89 =$ _____ $86 \times 88 =$ _____

2. $312 \times 57 =$ _____ $302 \times 67 =$ _____

3. $1{,}704 + 3{,}060 =$ _____ $1{,}086 + 3{,}704 =$ _____

4. $3{,}079 - 2{,}076 =$ _____ $3{,}790 - 2{,}767 =$ _____

5. $83 + 124 + 764 =$ _____ $384 + 345 + 96 =$ _____

6. $8{,}424 \div 39 =$ _____ $8{,}232 \div 42 =$ _____

7. $36 \times 89 =$ _____ $52 \times 68 =$ _____

8. $316 - 89 =$ _____ $328 - 109 =$ _____

9. $1{,}445 \div 17 =$ _____ $1{,}596 \div 19 =$ _____

10. $1{,}007 - 447 =$ _____ $987 - 394 =$ _____

11. Round the answers you have circled in column A to the nearest ten. Estimate the sum.

12. Round each answer you have circled in column B to the nearest hundred. Estimate the sum.

13. Complete: "My answer to number 12 is about _____ times my answer to number 11."

NAME _____   DATE _____

1–6 THE TRIO ROUNDS TO . . .

In each of the following sets of numbers, three of the numbers can be rounded to the same number. One cannot. Circle the three numbers that can be rounded to the same number, and write your answers in the spaces provided.

Rounded Number

1. 15   24   18   25   _____

2. 158   175   149   151   _____

3. 12   9   15   8   _____

4. 254   284   309   365   _____

5. 991   943   985   989   _____

6. 550   1,755   1,358   1,059   _____

7. 750   801   907   843   _____

8. 3,481   3,505   3,516   3,416   _____

9. 1,850   2,459   1,999   2,501   _____

10. 2,497   2,479   2,551   2,515   _____

NAME _____   DATE _____

1-7 A FACT ABOUT YOU

Answer each question and find your answer in the Answer Bank. Write the letter of your answer in the space provided before each problem. Then read down the column to discover a fact that applies to you. Some answers will be used more than once; some answers will not be used.

1. _____ It has the fewest factors of any number.

2. _____ It is the smallest number that has only two factors.

3. _____ This one-digit number has the same number of factors as the number 6.

4. _____ It is the smallest number that has six factors.

5. _____ It is the smallest three-digit perfect square.

6. _____ It is the smallest three-digit number that has only two factors.

7. _____ It is the largest two-digit perfect square that has three factors.

8. _____ It is the smallest three-digit perfect square that has nine factors.

9. _____ The factors of this number are 1, 2, 3, 4, 6, and 12.

10. _____ This perfect square is the same as a gross.

11. _____ It is a factor of half of all the numbers.

12. _____ It is the smallest perfect square that has nine factors.

Answer Bank

D. 121	N. 101	E. 16	K. 90	F. 49
U. 8	Y. 1	C. 12	O. 2	M. 80
B. 9	R. 36	T. 144	S. 4	A. 100

NAME _____ DATE _____

1-8 WHO AM I?

Answer the questions. Write your answers in the spaces provided.

1. I am the largest one-digit prime number. _____

2. I am the smallest two-digit prime number. _____

3. I have only one factor. _____

4. I am the only even prime number. _____

5. I am the largest two-digit prime number. _____

6. The number 59 and I are the only two prime numbers between 50 and 60. _____

7. If I am the units digit of any number, then the number is divisible by 10. _____

8. I am not the number 1, but I am a factor of 60 and 35. _____

9. I am a one-digit number. If you add all of my factors, the sum equals 12. _____

10. I am the largest one-digit number that has only three factors. _____

11. I am the first prime number after 100. _____

12. I am the largest composite number before 100. _____

NAME _____   DATE _____

1-9 WHICH ONE DOES NOT BELONG?

In each set of numbers, one number does not belong. Circle this number and explain why it does not belong with the others. (Consider such things as primes, composites, factors, and even spelling!) Then replace the number that does not belong with a number that does.

1. 2, 4, 7, 10 _____

    _____

2. 3, 5, 7, 9 _____

    _____

3. 12, 20, 26, 38 _____

    _____

4. 3, 4, 6, 9 _____

    _____

5. 2, 6, 12, 20 _____

    _____

6. 15, 20, 35, 85 _____

    _____

7. 9, 16, 20, 25 _____

    _____

8. 313, 1001, 111, 1313 _____

    _____

9. 3, 13, 31, 47 _____

    _____

10. 28, 30, 31, 32 _____

    _____

NAME _____ DATE _____

1-10 CROSS NUMBER PUZZLE: WHOLE NUMBERS

Use the following clues to solve the puzzle.

Across

1. 36 + 98

3. 6 less than item 1 Across

5. The product of 76 and 4

7. 3,690 divided by 5

8. 29 less than a thousand

11. The largest palindrome less than 900

13. $5 \times 10^3 + 2 \times 10^2 + 8 \times 10^1 + 7 \times 10^0$

14. 16 less than item 13 Across

16. 8×10^2

17. 52 times the largest prime number that is less than 20

Down

2. The next odd number after 301

4. 38 times 76

6. 7 squared

7. The next prime number after 67

9. 1,287 − 548

10. 369 + 584 + 287

11. 3,132 ÷ 36

12. 340 ÷ 4

15. The product of 118 and 6

NAME _____ DATE _____

1–11 THE POWERS OF PRIMES

Use the prime numbers 2, 3, 5, 7, and 11. Choose a base and an exponent from these numbers to equal the number in each problem. The first problem is done for you.

Work Space

1. $25 = \underline{\ 5^2\ }$

2. $8 = \underline{\hspace{2cm}}$

3. $27 = \underline{\hspace{2cm}}$

4. $32 = \underline{\hspace{2cm}}$

5. $49 = \underline{\hspace{2cm}}$

6. $125 = \underline{\hspace{2cm}}$

7. $4 = \underline{\hspace{2cm}}$

8. $9 = \underline{\hspace{2cm}}$

9. $343 = \underline{\hspace{2cm}}$

10. $243 = \underline{\hspace{2cm}}$

11. $121 = \underline{\hspace{2cm}}$

12. $2,048 = \underline{\hspace{2cm}}$

NAME _____ DATE _____

1–12 CUBES AND SQUARES

Find the numbers related to squares and cubes.

1. Find the only one-digit number that is both a square number and a cubic number. _____

2. Find the only two-digit number that is both a square number and a cubic number. _____

3. Find the only three-digit number that is both a square number and a cubic number. _____

4. Find a two-digit number that is one more than a square number and one less than a cubic number. _____

5. Find the smallest two-digit square number that can be written as the sum of two square numbers. _____

6. Find the smallest three-digit square number that is the sum of two square numbers. _____

7. Find the only one-digit number that can be written as the sum of two different cubic numbers. _____

8. Find the smallest two-digit number that can be written as the sum of two cubic numbers. _____

9. Find the largest two-digit number that can be written as the sum of two different cubic numbers. _____

10. Find a two-digit number that is one less than a square number, and when doubled is one less than a square number. _____

NAME _____ DATE _____

1-13 AN EXPONENTIAL TYPO

In the equations below, every exponent that should have been raised was instead placed on the line by a careless typist. All of the other symbols are correct. Circle the exponent, or exponents, in each equation that should have been raised in order to correct the equation. Then rewrite the equations correctly.

Work Space

1. $23 + 74 = 82$

2. $92 - (3 + 6)2 = 11$

3. $24 \div 23 = 2$

4. $(3 + 5)2 - 62 - 7 \times 22 = 0$

5. $52 = 16 + 24$

6. $23 \div 4 = 21$

7. $24 = 6 \times 22 - 23$

8. $36 + 82 = 102$

9. $32 = 20 + 23$

10. $42 + 36 - 70 = 77$

NAME _____ DATE _____

1-14 EUCLID AND THE GCF

More than two thousand years ago, Euclid, the Greek mathematician, devised a method to find the GCF (greatest common factor) of two numbers. You can use this method today. Just follow these steps:

1. **Divide the larger number by the smaller number.**

2. **Divide the smaller number by the remainder in the first step.**

3. **Repeat this process until there is no remainder.**

4. **The last divisor is the GCF of the original numbers.**

Here is an example. Find the GCF of 224 and 78. Follow Euclid's steps:

1. **Divide 224 by 78. The answer is 2 R68.**

2. **Divide 78 by 68. The answer is 1 R10.**

3. **Divide 68 by 10. The answer is 6 R8.**

4. **Divide 10 by 8. The answer is 1 R2.**

5. **Divide 8 by 2. The answer is 4; 2 is the GCF.**

Use Euclid's method to find the GCF of each pair of numbers.

1. 105, 27   GCF = _____

2. 40, 27   GCF = _____

3. 84, 72   GCF = _____

4. 98, 134   GCF = _____

5. 51, 217   GCF = _____

6. 105, 78   GCF = _____

7. 82, 96   GCF = _____

8. 333, 96   GCF = _____

9. 150, 215   GCF = _____

10. 240, 179   GCF = _____

NAME _____ DATE _____

1-15 FINDING THE LCM USING THE GCF

A way to find the LCM (least common multiple) of two or more numbers is to find the product of the numbers and then divide the product by the GCF (greatest common factor). Use this method to find the LCM of each group of numbers below.

Work Space

1. 36, 80   LCM = _____

2. 24, 86   LCM = _____

3. 70, 45   LCM = _____

4. 54, 64   LCM = _____

5. 93, 60   LCM = _____

6. 62, 88   LCM = _____

7. 49, 27   LCM = _____

8. 38, 46   LCM = _____

9. 12, 45, 63   LCM = _____

10. 56, 12, 16   LCM = _____

NAME _____   DATE _____

1–16 THE MISSING SYMBOLS

Place addition, subtraction, multiplication, or division signs to make each expression correct. For some equations, you may also need to insert parentheses. Write the revised equations in the work space.

Work Space

1. 8   2   6   3 = 14

2. 3   2   6   4 = 32

3. 16   4   6   1 = 10

4. 9   8   3   2 = 7

5. 3   3   2   3 = 1

6. 12   3   2   2 = 0

7. 7   4   1   3 = 9

8. 1   8   6   3 = 1

9. 15   5   3   7 = 2

10. 15   3   4   8 = 11

NAME _____ DATE _____

1–17 WHAT A MIX-UP!

The problems below are missing their problem numbers and are out of order. Solve the problems, and write the correct problem number before each. (Remember to follow the order of operations.)

Work Space

_____ $9 + 5 - (1 + 4)$

_____ $10 \div 2 + 8 \div 4$

_____ $10 \div (2 + 8) + 3$

_____ $4 \times 2 - 3 \times 1$

_____ $(4 + 3 \times 2) \div 5$

_____ $8 - 1 \times 5 + 7$

_____ $10 - (8 + 1) + 5$

_____ $2(3 + 4) - 4 \times 3 - 1$

_____ $2(3 + 4) - (4 \times 3 - 1)$

_____ $10 - 2 \times 4 + 6(9 - 8)$

DATE

1–18 A PERFECT 10

Using the digits 2, 4, 6, and 8, create equations with answers ranging from 1 to 10. You may use addition, subtraction, multiplication, and division. You may also use parentheses. You must use each digit once (and only once!) in each problem.

Here is an example: $1 = (8 - 4) \div (6 - 2)$. Start by finding an equation of your own to equal 1, and then continue.

1 = _____

2 = _____

3 = _____

4 = _____

5 = _____

6 = _____

7 = _____

8 = _____

9 = _____

10 = _____

NAME _____ DATE _____

1–19 NOT-SO-FAMOUS FIRSTS FOR PRESIDENTS

Simplify the expression beneath the name of the president, and write your answer in the space provided. Match your answers to the numbers in the Fact Bank to learn an interesting fact about these men.

1. John Adams
   $13 - 4 \times 2 =$ _____

2. John Quincy Adams
   $(8 - 3) \times 5 =$ _____

3. Martin Van Buren
   $6 + 3 \times 4 =$ _____

4. William Henry Harrison
   $28 - 3 \times 5 =$ _____

5. John Tyler
   $(8 + 4) \div 4 =$ _____

6. Millard Fillmore
   $13 \times 2 - 3 \times 4 =$ _____

7. Abraham Lincoln
   $(9 + 4) \times 2 =$ _____

8. Grover Cleveland
   $40 \div 2 \times 4 - 3 =$ _____

9. William H. Taft
   $7 + 9 \times 3 + 2 =$ _____

10. Woodrow Wilson
    $7 \times 8 - 5 \times 3 =$ _____

11. Herbert C. Hoover
    $45 - 7 \times 5 - 4 =$ _____

12. Dwight D. Eisenhower
    $3 \times 6 - 2 =$ _____

Fact Bank

13 president who had the shortest presidency
25 first president to have his photo taken
36 first president to throw out the first pitch to start the baseball season
 5 first president to live in the White House
14 president who started the White House library
16 first president to have a pilot's license
77 candy bar Baby Ruth named to honor this president's daughter
26 first president to patent an invention
 3 president who had the most children
 6 asteroid was named for this president
41 first president to speak on the radio
18 first president to be born a U.S. citizen, not a British subject

NAME _____ DATE _____

1-20 WHAT'S NEXT?

Find the missing numbers to complete the patterns.

1. 5, _____, _____, 8, _____, 10

2. 1, 2, _____, _____, _____, 32

3. 9, 8, _____, _____, _____, 4

4. 0, _____, _____, 15, _____, 25

5. 2, _____, _____, _____, 11, 13

6. _____, _____, 9, 16, _____, 36

7. 9, _____, _____, 18, 21, _____

8. _____, 240, 120, _____, 30, _____

9. 2, 5, 11, _____, _____, _____

10. 4, _____, _____, 10, _____, 19

Section 1: Whole Numbers

NAME _____ DATE _____

1-21 NUMBERS OF ALL KINDS

All of the words below relate to some type of number. Use the clues to unscramble these "number" words. Read carefully!

1. **smtocoipe:** having three or more factors _____

2. **starofc:** 4 has three of these _____

3. **veen:** can be divided by 2 _____

4. **erufigat:** in great shape _____

5. **ntadunab:** plentiful _____

6. **imrep:** having only two factors _____

7. **suliptmel:** every number has these _____

8. **dod:** peculiar _____

9. **minadepolr:** can also be a word or phrase _____

10. **ehwlo:** complete _____

11. **fereptc:** far better than good _____

12. **ceindieft:** lacking in some way _____

13. **preim:** backwards prime _____

14. **ialndarc:** a red bird _____

15. **tulanar:** not artificial _____

NAME _____   DATE _____

1–22   VAL'S BABY-SITTING JOB

Complete the story by filling in the blanks with the correct numbers.

Valerie sat in the school cafeteria and noticed that it was eleven o'clock. At 7:00 P.M.,
just _____ hours from now, she would begin baby-sitting the two daughters of her neigh-
bor, Mrs. Taylor. Mrs. Taylor offered to pay Val $3 per hour for each girl. Since Mrs. Taylor
planned to be back about 11:00 P.M., Val figured that she would earn a total of $_____ for
the night.

Val arrived at the Taylor house at 6:45 P.M., _____ minutes ahead of time. Sarah, Mrs.
Taylor's older daughter, was visiting a friend and did not return home until nine o'clock.
Val watched Erin, the younger daughter, from 7:00 until 11:00 and watched Sarah from 9:00
to 11:00.

Including a $3 tip, Mrs. Taylor paid Val $_____. This was $_____ less than Val had
expected to earn, but she did not have to watch both girls as long as she had thought. Before
she left, Mrs. Taylor asked Val if she could watch the girls next Saturday from 6:30 P.M. until
12:30 A.M. She would pay Val the same rate for a total of $_____.

As Val left, she thought about the things she could buy with the $_____, the total
amount of money she expected to earn for the two nights of baby-sitting.

NAME _____ DATE _____

1–23   IS THE PRICE RIGHT?

The owners of the stores in Skattersville, a somewhat unusual town, price their goods in an unusual way. The consonants and vowels in the name of an item have a monetary value. The cost of an item is found by multiplying the number of consonants in the name of the item by the value of the consonants, and then adding the product of the number of vowels and the value of the vowels. For example, if consonants were worth \$1 and vowels were worth \$2, the cost of an *eraser* would be \$9.

Find the value of the third item in the problems that follow.

1.   If a book costs \$12 and a pencil costs \$22, a pen costs _____.

2.   If a pair of sneakers costs \$19 and a pair of socks costs \$11, shorts cost _____.

3.   If a newspaper costs \$27 and a magazine costs \$20, a book costs _____.

4.   If a protractor costs \$17 and a ruler costs \$8, a compass costs _____.

5.   If an apple costs \$17 and an orange costs \$21, a plum costs _____.

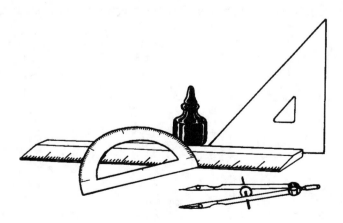

Section 2

FRACTIONS, DECIMALS, AND PERCENTS

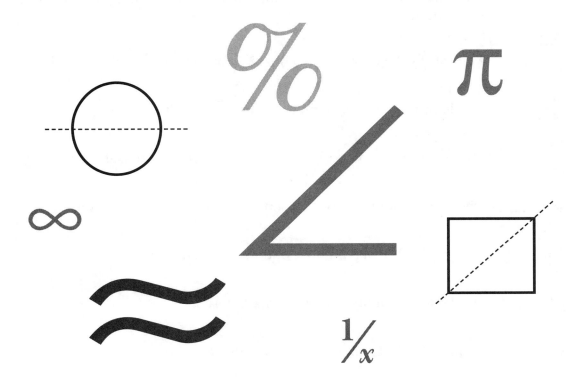

NAME _____ DATE _____

2–1 FRACTIONAL TRIVIA

Multiply or divide the numerator and denominator of each fraction by the number provided in the clue to find an equivalent fraction.

1. $\frac{3}{8}$ = _____ Multiply by the number of singers in a trio.

2. $\frac{8}{16}$ = _____ Divide by the number of seasons in a year.

3. $\frac{7}{9}$ = _____ Multiply by the number of faces of a cube.

4. $\frac{36}{60}$ = _____ Divide by the number of months in a year.

5. $\frac{6}{7}$ = _____ Multiply by the number of innings in a baseball game. (Do not consider extra innings.)

6. $\frac{7}{12}$ = _____ Multiply by the number of players in a basketball team's starting lineup.

7. $\frac{40}{56}$ = _____ Divide by the number of months that have 30 days.

8. $\frac{12}{15}$ = _____ Multiply by the number you fear if you suffer from triskaidekaphobia.

9. $\frac{12}{18}$ = _____ Divide by the number of U.S. senators who represent your state.

10. $\frac{7}{8}$ = _____ Multiply by the total number of dots on a pair of dice.

11. $\frac{24}{96}$ = _____ Divide by the number of sides on a stop sign.

12. $\frac{8}{11}$ = _____ Multiply by the number of letters of the alphabet.

NAME _____ DATE _____

2-2 ODD FRACTION OUT

In each set of fractions, one fraction is not equivalent to the other three. Circle this fraction, then replace it with a fraction from the Fraction Bank that is equivalent to the others in the set. Write this fraction on the line.

1. $\dfrac{9}{15}$ $\dfrac{6}{8}$ $\dfrac{3}{5}$ $\dfrac{21}{35}$ _____

2. $\dfrac{4}{6}$ $\dfrac{2}{3}$ $\dfrac{7}{8}$ $\dfrac{12}{18}$ _____

3. $\dfrac{2}{9}$ $\dfrac{16}{72}$ $\dfrac{14}{63}$ $\dfrac{12}{90}$ _____

4. $\dfrac{12}{15}$ $\dfrac{20}{25}$ $\dfrac{16}{20}$ $\dfrac{28}{30}$ _____

5. $\dfrac{28}{32}$ $\dfrac{21}{24}$ $\dfrac{49}{56}$ $\dfrac{14}{18}$ _____

6. $\dfrac{9}{21}$ $\dfrac{6}{14}$ $\dfrac{12}{27}$ $\dfrac{30}{70}$ _____

7. $\dfrac{10}{12}$ $\dfrac{25}{36}$ $\dfrac{25}{30}$ $\dfrac{40}{48}$ _____

8. $\dfrac{9}{15}$ $\dfrac{12}{16}$ $\dfrac{33}{44}$ $\dfrac{21}{28}$ _____

9. $\dfrac{14}{22}$ $\dfrac{84}{132}$ $\dfrac{49}{121}$ $\dfrac{56}{88}$ _____

10. $\dfrac{15}{36}$ $\dfrac{35}{84}$ $\dfrac{10}{60}$ $\dfrac{20}{48}$ _____

Fraction Bank

$\dfrac{12}{28}$ $\dfrac{20}{30}$ $\dfrac{55}{66}$ $\dfrac{8}{10}$ $\dfrac{10}{45}$

$\dfrac{49}{77}$ $\dfrac{6}{10}$ $\dfrac{60}{144}$ $\dfrac{42}{48}$ $\dfrac{18}{24}$

NAME _____   DATE _____

2–3   DON'T BE REDUNDANT

Some of the problems below are correct. For those that are, write *correct*. For those that are incorrect, rewrite them so that they are correct.

1. $\dfrac{7}{8} = 0.87$

2. $\dfrac{3}{10} = 0.3$

3. $\dfrac{5}{9} = 0.5$

4. $\dfrac{1}{6} = 0.16$

5. $\dfrac{3}{11} = 0.27$

6. $\dfrac{5}{7} = 0.714$

7. $\dfrac{2}{99} = 0.\overline{02}$

8. $\dfrac{1}{25} = 0.04$

9. $\dfrac{5}{33} = 0.15$

10. $\dfrac{4}{27} = 0.14\overline{8}$

11. $\dfrac{3}{40} = 0.075$

12. $\dfrac{15}{18} = 0.83$

13. $\dfrac{9}{25} = 0.36$

14. $\dfrac{25}{90} = 0.27$

15. $\dfrac{3}{48} = 0.062$

NAME _____ DATE _____

2-4 OUT OF ORDER

All of the fractions in each set are supposed to be in ascending order, but at least one of the fractions in each set is out of order. Rewrite each set so that the fractions are in ascending order.

1. $\frac{7}{25}$ $\frac{7}{20}$ $\frac{3}{10}$ $\frac{9}{25}$ _____

2. $\frac{1}{3}$ $\frac{3}{4}$ $\frac{2}{5}$ $\frac{1}{2}$ _____

3. $\frac{4}{5}$ $\frac{9}{10}$ $\frac{8}{9}$ $\frac{7}{8}$ _____

4. $\frac{1}{4}$ $\frac{19}{50}$ $\frac{1}{2}$ $\frac{49}{100}$ _____

5. $\frac{3}{4}$ $\frac{4}{5}$ $\frac{5}{7}$ $\frac{8}{9}$ _____

6. $\frac{1}{3}$ $\frac{3}{8}$ $\frac{4}{7}$ $\frac{4}{9}$ _____

7. $\frac{7}{9}$ $\frac{3}{4}$ $\frac{5}{8}$ $\frac{11}{15}$ _____

8. $\frac{5}{13}$ $\frac{2}{9}$ $\frac{1}{5}$ $\frac{3}{11}$ _____

9. $\frac{5}{11}$ $\frac{4}{9}$ $\frac{3}{5}$ $\frac{7}{8}$ _____

10. $\frac{2}{3}$ $\frac{4}{5}$ $\frac{7}{8}$ $\frac{9}{11}$ _____

NAME _____   DATE _____

2-5 DON'T BE SQUARE

A number is described in each portion of the chart below. Write these numbers in the circles within the portions to create a magic square. If you are correct, the sum of the numbers you have written in each row, column, and diagonal should equal 68.

The LCD of $\frac{3}{4}$ and $\frac{1}{6}$ =	The LCD of $\frac{7}{8}$ and $\frac{2}{3}$ =	The GCF of 4 and 10 =	The LCD of $\frac{7}{30}$ and $\frac{1}{10}$ =
◯	◯	◯	◯
The LCD of $\frac{5}{6}$ and $\frac{2}{9}$ =	The GCF of 28 and 42 =	The LCD of $\frac{3}{14}$ and $\frac{1}{4}$ =	The LCD of $\frac{3}{4}$ and $\frac{7}{8}$ =
◯	◯	◯	◯
The LCD of $\frac{7}{8}$ and $\frac{5}{32}$ =	The GCF of 20 and 36 =	The LCD of $\frac{1}{11}$ and $\frac{1}{2}$ =	The LCD of $\frac{1}{10}$ and $\frac{1}{5}$ =
◯	◯	◯	◯
The GCF of 18 and 30 =	The GCF of 26 and 52 =	The LCD of $\frac{7}{16}$ and $\frac{1}{4}$ =	The LCD of $\frac{3}{4}$ and $\frac{9}{10}$ =
◯	◯	◯	◯

NAME _____   DATE _____

2-6 BOXES AND NUMBERS

Complete the problems by filling in each box with the numbers 2, 4, 6, or 8 to find the answer described on the right. Use only proper fractions in the problems and answers. Each number must be used once in each problem.

1. $\dfrac{\Box}{\Box} + \dfrac{\Box}{\Box} =$ largest sum

2. $\dfrac{\Box}{\Box} + \dfrac{\Box}{\Box} =$ smallest sum

3. $\dfrac{\Box}{\Box} - \dfrac{\Box}{\Box} =$ largest difference

4. $\dfrac{\Box}{\Box} - \dfrac{\Box}{\Box} =$ smallest difference

5. $\dfrac{\Box}{\Box} \times \dfrac{\Box}{\Box} =$ largest product

6. $\dfrac{\Box}{\Box} \times \dfrac{\Box}{\Box} =$ smallest product

7. $\dfrac{\Box}{\Box} \div \dfrac{\Box}{\Box} =$ largest quotient

8. $\dfrac{\Box}{\Box} \div \dfrac{\Box}{\Box} =$ smallest quotient

Section 2: Fractions, Decimals, and Percents   **31**

2-7 THINK ABOUT THIS

Find the fractions described below. For some problems, there may be more than one answer, but you need only give one. (Remember that whole numbers may also be written as fractions with a denominator of 1.)

1. Find two fractions. Their product is less than their sum.

2. Find two fractions. Their quotient is larger than their difference.

3. Find a fraction that is equal to its reciprocal.

4. Find two different fractions with a numerator of 1 that have the largest sum.

5. Find a fraction that can be expressed as a repeating decimal, but whose reciprocal terminates.

6. Find a simplified fraction and its reciprocal that both can be expressed as terminating decimals.

7. Find two proper fractions whose sum, difference, product, and quotient are between 0 and 1.

8. Find two improper fractions whose sum and product are greater than 1, and whose difference and quotient are less than 1.

9. Find three fractions whose sum is less than 1.

10. Find three simplified fractions whose sum is 1.

NAME _____ DATE _____

2-8 FILLING IN FRACTIONS

Complete each problem by filling in the boxes with 2, 4, 6, or 8 to make the problem correct. Each number must be used once in each problem.

1. $5\dfrac{\square}{\square} + 3\dfrac{\square}{\square} = 9\dfrac{1}{4}$

4. $3\dfrac{\square}{\square} \times 1\dfrac{\square}{\square} = 4\dfrac{7}{12}$

2. $7\dfrac{3}{\square} - \square\dfrac{\square}{\square} = 3\dfrac{1}{4}$

5. $\square\dfrac{\square}{\square} \div \square = \dfrac{5}{12}$

3. $3\dfrac{\square}{\square} - 1\dfrac{\square}{\square} = 1\dfrac{7}{12}$

6. $\square\dfrac{\square}{\square} \div \square\dfrac{1}{3} = \dfrac{39}{50}$

NAME _____   DATE _____

2–9   MAKING A MATCH

Each value on the left can be matched with a value in the Answer Bank on the right. Write the letter of the answer in the blank in front of the problem. When you are done, read down the column to find a fact about you.

1. _____ $3\frac{2}{3}$

2. _____ $\frac{3}{4} + \frac{1}{2}$

3. _____ $3\frac{7}{8} - \frac{5}{12}$

4. _____ $\frac{2}{3} \cdot 1\frac{5}{6}$

5. _____ $1\frac{3}{4} \times 2\frac{1}{2}$

6. _____ $\frac{10}{6}$

7. _____ $5\frac{3}{4} \div 2\frac{1}{4}$

8. _____ $6\frac{1}{2} \div 5\frac{1}{5}$

9. _____ $1\frac{7}{8} + 2\frac{1}{2}$

10. _____ $\frac{35}{8}$

11. _____ $7\frac{1}{2} \cdot \frac{2}{9}$

12. _____ $1\frac{2}{9} + 1\frac{1}{3}$

13. _____ $2\frac{1}{4} - \frac{2}{3}$

Answer Bank

C. $2\frac{5}{9}$

T. $1\frac{7}{12}$

U. $3\frac{11}{24}$

R. $4\frac{3}{8}$

E. $1\frac{2}{3}$

Y. $\frac{11}{3}$

O. $1\frac{1}{4}$

A. $1\frac{2}{9}$

NAME _____ DATE _____

2-10 NOT REALLY COMPLEX AT ALL

Simplify each complex fraction.

1. $\dfrac{\frac{3}{4}}{\frac{1}{2}} =$

2. $\dfrac{\frac{2}{9}}{\frac{1}{5}} =$

3. $\dfrac{\frac{4}{5}}{\frac{2}{15}} =$

4. $\dfrac{2}{\frac{1}{7}} =$

5. $\dfrac{\frac{3}{5}}{6} =$

6. $\dfrac{1\frac{5}{6}}{\frac{2}{9}} =$

7. $\dfrac{3\frac{1}{8}}{2\frac{1}{5}} =$

8. $\dfrac{2\frac{3}{4}}{1\frac{1}{6}} =$

For problems 9 through 12, supply the missing fraction to make the statement true.

9. $\dfrac{\frac{3}{8}}{?} = \frac{1}{5}$

10. $\dfrac{?}{3} = \frac{7}{27}$

11. $\dfrac{\frac{3}{5}}{?} = \frac{9}{20}$

12. $\dfrac{?}{2\frac{1}{4}} = \frac{44}{45}$

NAME _____ DATE _____

2-11 MAKING A POINT

Insert a decimal point in each decimal so that the statement is correct.

1. 16398   3 is in the tenths place

2. 37268   2 is in the hundredths place

3. 95146   5 is in the ones place

4. 87143   4 is in the thousandths place

5. 38579   7 is in the tenths place

6. 72468   7 is in the hundreds place

7. 92537   9 is in the thousands place

8. 671845   4 is in the ten-thousandths place

9. 594237   4 is in the hundreds place

10. 593148   1 is in the hundredths place

11. 923468   6 is in the ones place

12. 4637495   6 is in the ten-thousands place

13. 4528605   8 is in the tens place

14. 6431298   2 is in the thousandths place

15. 5398712   5 is in the tenths place

NAME _____ DATE _____

2-12 MORE OR LESS

Express each quantity as a decimal. For example, 30 minutes = one half of an hour, or 0.5 hour. Compare each quantity in the left column with the quantity on the right. Then write >, <, or = to show the comparison. The first one is done for you.

1. 12 inches $\frac{1}{2}$ yard   _____ $0.\overline{3} < 0.5$ _____

2. 10 minutes $\frac{1}{4}$ hour   _____

3. 4 hours $\frac{1}{6}$ day   _____

4. 8 dimes $\frac{3}{4}$ dollar   _____

5. 9 inches $\frac{1}{4}$ yard   _____

6. 4 ounces $\frac{1}{3}$ pound   _____

7. 2 digits $\frac{2}{3}$ of an area code   _____

8. 4 fluid ounces $\frac{1}{2}$ cup   _____

9. 15 centimeters $1\frac{1}{2}$ meters   _____

10. 8 small squares $\frac{1}{4}$ of a checkerboard   _____

11. 7 zodiac signs $\frac{5}{6}$ of the zodiac   _____

12. 3 eggs $\frac{1}{6}$ of a dozen   _____

Section 2: Fractions, Decimals, and Percents

NAME _____ DATE _____

2–13 WHAT COMES FIRST?

Each decimal below is followed by the name of a toy or game. Arrange the decimals in order from least to greatest. You will then find the correct order in which these "timeless" toys and games were first produced.

1. **0.6** Raggedy Ann doll _____

2. **5.8** skateboards _____

3. **1.36** Monopoly _____

4. **6.8** Tickle Me Elmo _____

5. **0.13** baseball cards _____

6. **5.0** G.I. Joe _____

7. **1.3** Yo-Yo _____

8. **5.8102** Teenage Mutant Ninja Turtles _____

9. **2.14** Frisbee _____

10. **5.83** Rollerblades _____

11. **2.403** Barbie doll _____

12. **5.81** Cabbage Patch Kids doll _____

13. **0.1352** Ping-Pong _____

14. **1.74** Silly Putty _____

15. **0.136** Teddy bears _____

16. **6.08** Beanie Babies _____

17. **1** miniature golf _____

18. **0.52** jigsaw puzzles _____

19. **1.632** Scrabble _____

20. **2.41** Easy Bake Oven _____

NAME _____ DATE _____

2-14 WHAT'S THE POINT?

Express each decimal as a fraction. Write it beneath an equivalent fraction that is graphed on the number line at the bottom of the page.

1. $3.5 =$ _____   2. $0.75 =$ _____

3. $1.75 =$ _____   4. $3.\bar{5} =$ _____

5. $0.\bar{3} =$ _____   6. $2.1 =$ _____

7. $0.5 =$ _____   8. $1.1 =$ _____

9. $2.2 =$ _____   10. $0.\bar{1} =$ _____

11. $3.875 =$ _____   12. $3.125 =$ _____

13. $1.\bar{6} =$ _____   14. $2.8\bar{3} =$ _____

NAME _____ DATE _____

2-15 DECIMAL ROUND-UP

In each set of numbers all except one can be rounded to the same place. Round each of the numbers, and circle the one that cannot be rounded to the same place as the others. Write your answers on the line beneath each set of numbers.

1. 0.25   0.31   0.35   0.342

   _____

2. 0.322   0.324   0.333   0.315

   _____

3. 8.76   8.84   8.95   8.41

   _____

4. 37.152   38.152   37.9   37.54

   _____

5. 150.352   150.41   150.393   150.45

   _____

6. 1.3 $1.\overline{3}$ 1.375   1.295

   _____

7. $1.\overline{8}$ 1.84   1.89   1.932

   _____

8. 15.375   15.35   15.285   15.426

   _____

For problems 9 and 10, first change the fractions to decimals and then round. Circle the number that cannot be rounded to the same place as the others.

9. $\frac{1}{3}$ $\frac{1}{4}$ $\frac{1}{5}$ $\frac{5}{6}$

   _____

10. $3\frac{3}{8}$ $3\frac{4}{9}$ $3\frac{2}{5}$ $3\frac{7}{8}$

   _____

NAME _____ DATE _____

2–16 A DECIMAL CROSS NUMBER PUZZLE

Complete the cross number puzzle below. Place a decimal point in the small box within an answer if a decimal is necessary. Number 3 Across is done as an example.

Across

1. 1.8×27
3. $20 - 4.6$
5. 0.7×91
7. 0.21×6
8. $365.5 \div 17$
11. $6 - 0.21$
13. $0.493 + 0.983$
14. 41×0.58
16. $939.4 \div 11$
17. $72.87 \div 2.1$

Down

2. 0.59×14
4. 263.1×2
6. 0.8×0.9
7. $0.8 + 0.7$
9. $15.8 - 3.1$
10. 1.5×2.27
11. $5.6 \div 0.1$
12. 23×4
15. $0.019 + 0.695$

NAME _____ DATE _____

2-17 THE MISSING LINK

Find the missing link in each decimal chain.

1. Start with 8.5, add 3.6, subtract 10.5, divide by 0.4 = _____

2. Start with 25.8, divide by 0.3, multiply by 0.2, divide by 0.32 = _____

3. Start with 3.58, add _____, add 3.72, subtract 7 = 2.98

4. Start with _____, multiply by 0.18, subtract 0.568, multiply by 0.5 = 2.956

5. Start with 3.2, multiply by 3.6, multiply by 4.8, subtract _____ = 50.338

6. Start with _____, multiply by 0.9, divide by 0.3, multiply by 0.27 = 0.729

7. Start with 6.5, add _____, add 3.5, multiply by 0.12 = 2.064

8. Start with 2.6, add 3.8, subtract 2.9, divide by _____ = 5

9. Start with 1.5, divide by 0.3, subtract _____, multiply by 0.2 = 0.1

10. Start with _____, divide by 4, subtract 0.987, multiply by 5 = 2.39

NAME _____ DATE _____

2-18 GET THE POINT

The decimal points and one or more signs (+, −, ×, and ÷) have been omitted in each equation below. Rewrite each equation, inserting the decimal points and signs to make the equation true. You will *not* need to use parentheses, but you may need to include zeroes to indicate the correct value of a decimal.

1. 452   375 = 41.45   _____

2. 962   25 = 2.405   _____

3. 756   32 = 23.625   _____

4. 68   245 = 31.3   _____

5. 56   25 = 22.4   _____

6. 469   2132 = 255.8   _____

7. 2   123 = 0.246   _____

8. 24   12   702 = 9.02   _____

9. 75   345   23 = 10.72   _____

10. 164   40   382 = 15.662   _____

NAME _____   DATE _____

2–19 AT THE MALL

Solve each problem below. Write your answers on the line beneath the problem.

1. Sam bought two CDs. Each cost the same amount. He paid with two $20 bills and received $8.02 in change. Find the cost of each CD.

2. Four of Simone's friends have a birthday this month. Greeting cards are on sale. If three cards are bought, a fourth card is free. The three cards Simone chose cost $2.29, $2.59, and $2.99 each. Since the fourth card was free, what was the average cost of the four cards? (Round your answer to the nearest cent.)

3. T-shirts are on sale. If you purchase one, another of equal cost is half-price. Rob bought two T-shirts for a total cost of $17.97. Find the cost of one T-shirt.

4. A package of pens costs $0.10 more than two packages of pencils. A package of pens and a package of pencils costs $1.87. Find the cost of a package of pencils.

5. The pretzel stand in the mall sells one pretzel for $0.75. Danny saved $0.10 a pretzel when he bought three at a special price. What was this price?

6. Five girls decided to chip in and purchase a thank-you present for their dance instructor. Each girl contributed $5 for the gift, but they were $3.50 short. How much should each girl have contributed?

7. A pizza costs $11.99, plus $0.75 for each additional topping if three or more toppings are ordered. Otherwise, a topping costs $0.95. Find the cost per person if four people order a pizza with extra cheese and anchovies. (Round your answer to the nearest cent.)

8. Aisha went shopping and spent all but $1.51 of the money she earned baby-sitting. She worked for three hours at a rate of $4.50 per hour. How much money did she spend shopping?

NAME _____ DATE _____

2–20   DO YOU HAVE SOME CHANGE?

Juan purchased popcorn and soda at the movie theater. He paid with a $10 bill and received three bills of the same denomination and two coins in change. (He received no dollar coins and no half dollars.) How much did he spend? There are ten possible answers. Try to find them all.

1. _____   2. _____

3. _____   4. _____

5. _____   6. _____

7. _____   8. _____

9. _____   10. _____

Section 2: Fractions, Decimals, and Percents

45

NAME _____ DATE _____

2–21 HUMAN BODY STATISTICS

Write each italicized number fact about the human body in scientific notation.

1. According to one theory, most human beings live for about *2.4 billion* heartbeats.

   _____

2. The human body contains *75 trillion* cells. Each day *2 billion* cells die and are replaced.

   _____ _____

3. There are about *1.5* gallons of blood in men and *0.875* gallons in women.

   _____ _____

4. The adult human body has about *60,000* miles of blood vessels. _____

5. If the air sacs, or alveoli, in the lungs were flattened out, they would cover between *600* and *1,000* square feet. _____ _____

6. The human body responds to warmth and cold within *0.1* to *0.2* seconds.

   _____ _____

7. The reaction times for smell and pain are about *0.3* and *0.7* seconds. _____

   _____

8. Impulses can travel through the human nervous system as fast as *223* miles per hour.

   _____

Copyright © 2004 by Judith A. Muschla and Gary Robert Muschla

NAME _____ DATE _____

2–22 CELESTIAL FACTS

Write each number in standard form. Use the space below each equation for your answer.

1. **Mean distance from Mercury to the sun:** 3.6×10^7 miles =

2. **Mean distance from Earth to the sun:** 9.296×10^7 miles =

3. **Mean distance from the Moon to the Earth:** 2.4×10^5 miles =

4. **Mean distance from Pluto to the sun:** 3.666×10^9 miles =

5. **Sun's temperature at its core:** 2.7×10^7 ° F =

6. **Sun's temperature at its surface:** 8.7×10^3 ° F =

7. **Radius of the sun:** about 4.3×10^5 miles =

8. **Speed of light (in a vacuum):** about 1.86×10^5 miles per second =

2-23 RIGHT AND WRONG

Two of the problems in each row have the same answer. Find the solutions to the problems and identify the problem that has a different answer.

1. $\dfrac{1}{8} + \dfrac{1}{2} + \dfrac{3}{4} =$ $\dfrac{5}{7} \div 2 =$ $2\dfrac{7}{24} \times \dfrac{3}{5} =$

2. $\dfrac{3}{5} + \dfrac{3}{40} =$ $\dfrac{3}{40} \div \dfrac{1}{9} =$ $1\dfrac{9}{16} \times \dfrac{2}{5} =$

3. $3\dfrac{5}{6} + \dfrac{4}{9} =$ $15\dfrac{2}{5} \times \dfrac{5}{18} =$ $5\dfrac{5}{9} \div 1\dfrac{1}{3} =$

4. $3\dfrac{13}{40} \div 2\dfrac{1}{2} =$ $4\dfrac{5}{16} \div 2\dfrac{3}{10} =$ $7\dfrac{17}{24} - 5\dfrac{5}{6} =$

5. $0.6 \times 0.75 =$ $15 \times 0.3 =$ $0.9 \times 0.5 =$

6. $0.35 \times 24 =$ $3.5 \times 2.5 =$ $5.1 + 3.65 =$

7. $8.8 \div 2 =$ $1.6 + 2.8 =$ $11.8 - 7.5 =$

8. $3.5 - 2.378 =$ $5.76 \div 4.8 =$ $9.882 - 8.76 =$

NAME _____ DATE _____

2–24 MYSTERY RATIOS

Use the numbers 1 through 10 to answer the following questions. Express each ratio in simplest form.

1. Write the ratio of prime numbers to composite numbers. _____

2. Write the ratio of composite numbers to the numbers that are not prime. _____

3. Write the ratio of multiples of 3 to the multiples of 5. _____

4. Write the ratio of one-digit numbers to two-digit numbers. _____

5. Write the ratio of square numbers to numbers that have four factors. _____

6. Write the ratio of the numbers that are divisible by 7 to those that are divisible by 3. _____

7. Write the ratio of the sum of the even numbers to the sum of the odd numbers. _____

8. Write the ratio of the product of the even numbers to the product of the odd numbers. _____

9. Write the ratio of the sum of the even integers to the sum of all the integers. _____

10. Write the ratio of the number of factors of 8 to the number of factors of 4. _____

Section 2: Fractions, Decimals, and Percents

49

NAME _____ DATE _____

2–25   HOW DO YOU RATE?

Express each ratio in simplest terms. You may need to consult your math text or reference sources to answer some of the problems.

1. 2 to 10 _____

2. 2 feet to 1 yard _____

3. $0.50 to $2.50 _____

4. 2 feet to 6 inches _____

5. 1 centimeter : 5 meters _____

6. 1 quart to 1 gallon _____

7. 2 hours to 1 day _____

8. 1 egg : 1 dozen _____

9. 60 minutes : 1 hour _____

10. The ratio of the number of dimes in $1.00 to the number of nickels in $1.00. _____

11. The ratio of a 60° angle to its complement. _____

12. The ratio of boys to girls in a group of 25 people if 20 are girls. _____

13. The ratio of wins to losses of a team that won 15 out of 20 games and had no ties. _____

14. The ratio of the side of a square to its perimeter. _____

15. The ratio of correct answers to the total problems if a score is 100 percent. _____

NAME _____   DATE _____

2–26 WHAT'S COOKING?

Write a proportion and find the missing values for the problems below. Write your answers beneath the problems.

1. Eight slices of cooked bacon are equal to one-half cup of crumbled bacon. How many cups of crumbled bacon are equivalent to twelve slices of cooked bacon?

2. One and a half slices of bread with the crust are equal to a half cup of bread crumbs. About how many slices of bread are required if a recipe calls for one-quarter cup of bread crumbs?

3. Sixteen ounces of salad dressing are equal to two cups of dressing. Find the equivalent of twenty ounces of salad dressing.

4. One cup of molasses can be replaced with three-quarters of a cup of granulated sugar. How many cups of granulated sugar can be substituted if two cups of molasses are required?

5. One-quarter pound of Parmesan cheese is equal to one cup of grated cheese. How many pounds of Parmesan cheese are required if a recipe calls for one and one-third cups of grated cheese?

6. Fourteen square graham crackers are equal to one cup of fine crumbs. About how many crackers are needed if two-thirds of a cup of crumbs is required?

7. One pound of cake flour is equal to three and one-half cups of unsifted flour. How many cups of unsifted flour can be obtained from a five-pound box of cake flour?

8. One cup of dry macaroni is equal to two and one-half cups of cooked macaroni. How much dry macaroni is required in a recipe that calls for three cups of cooked macaroni?

NAME _____   DATE _____

2-27 FINDING THE THIRD

Two out of three equivalences (fraction, decimal, and percent) are included in each set of numbers below. Find the third equivalence. (Express fractions in simplest form.)

1. $\frac{1}{2}$ 0.5   _____

2. $\frac{5}{6}$ 83.$\overline{3}$%   _____

3. 0.8   80%   _____

4. 75% $\frac{3}{4}$ _____

5. $\frac{1}{3}$ 0.$\overline{3}$ _____

6. 55.$\overline{5}$% $\frac{5}{9}$ _____

7. 0.3 $\frac{3}{10}$ _____

8. 25%   0.25   _____

9. $66\frac{2}{3}$%   0.$\overline{6}$ _____

10. $\frac{1}{5}$ 0.2   _____

11. 0.125   12.5%   _____

12. $\frac{1}{16}$ 6.25%   _____

13. 0.375 $\frac{3}{8}$ _____

14. 90% $\frac{9}{10}$ _____

15. 16.$\overline{6}$%   0.1$\overline{6}$ _____

16. 70% $\frac{7}{10}$ _____

NAME _____   DATE _____

2-28 TIMES CHANGE

Solve each problem. By matching your answers with those in the Answer Bank, you will match the name of an occupation of the past with its modern equivalent. Write your answer and the modern occupation on the line next to each problem.

1. Find 27% of 50. _____
   (carter)

2. What percent of 80 is 44? _____
   (doorkeeper)

3. 20% of what number is 18? _____
   (coachman)

4. Find 75% of 24. _____
   (apothecarist)

5. 140 is what percent of 160? _____
   (cotter)

6. 80% of what number is 64? _____
   (fuller)

7. 140% of 85 is what number? _____
   (tinker)

8. $66\frac{2}{3}$% of 75 is what number? _____
   (vizier)

9. 45% of what number is 63? _____
   (bagger)

10. What percent of 12 is 54? _____
    (chiffonier)

Answer Bank

119 = handyman	13.5 = garbage collector	80 = cleaner	55 = security guard
50 = judge	18 = pharmacist	87.5 = groundskeeper	140 = porter
	90 = limousine driver	450 = secondhand clothes dealer	

NAME _____ DATE _____

2-29 PERCENTS WITH A TWIST

Solve each problem, using the given information.

1. 50% of 90 is the same as 40% of this number. _____

2. 30% of this number is the same as 15% of 40. _____

3. This percent of 35 is the same as 10% of 70. _____

4. 25% of 96 is the same as 15% of this number. _____

5. 18% of this number is the same as 8% of 90. _____

6. This percent of 36 is the same as 6.25% of 180. _____

7. 20% of 80 plus 20% of 50 is the same as 20% of this number. _____

8. 100% of 80 plus 80% of 100 equals this percent of 180. _____

NAME _____   DATE _____

2-30 SHORT WORK OF PERCENTS

Each method on the left describes a way to find the quantity on the right. Place the letter of this quantity in front of the problem number. (Most letters will be used more than once.) When you are done, read down the column to find your score.

1. _____ Divide the number by 5

2. _____ Multiply by $\frac{1}{4}$.

3. _____ Double the number.

4. _____ Divide the number by 3.

5. _____ Add the number to itself.

6. _____ Divide the number by 2.

7. _____ Multiply the number by 1.

8. _____ Multiply the number by 2.

9. _____ Multiply the number by $\frac{1}{2}$.

10. _____ Divide the number by 10.

11. _____ Multiply the number by 0.1.

12. _____ Do nothing.

13. _____ Multiply the number by $\frac{3}{2}$.

14. _____ Multiply the number by $\frac{5}{4}$.

15. _____ Divide the number by 4.

16. _____ Multiply the number by $\frac{1}{5}$.

E. 100% increase

L. 10% of the number

I. 50% increase

H. 25% of the number

A. 50% of the number

T. 20% of the number

R. 100% of the number

S. $33\frac{1}{3}$% of the number

G. 125% increase

Section 3

GEOMETRY

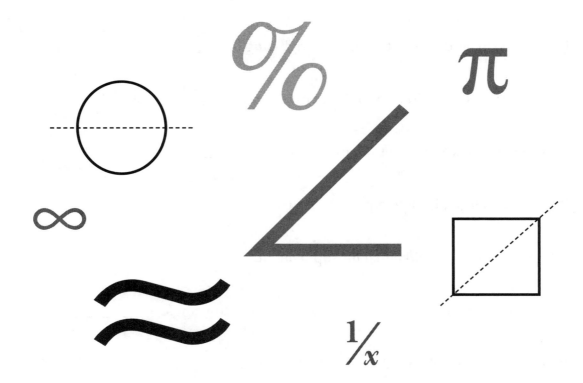

NAME _____ DATE _____

3-1   WHAT'S THE ANGLE?

Write the measure of each angle.

1. I am a right angle. _____

2. My complement is 15°. _____

3. My supplement is 125°. _____

4. I have no complement. _____

5. I am the supplement of a 50° angle. _____

6. If I were decreased by 15°, I would be a right angle. _____

7. If I were tripled, I would be a straight angle. _____

8. My supplement is 4 times my complement. _____

9. If I were 10° larger, I would equal my complement. _____

10. If I were 40° less, I would equal my supplement. _____

11. My measure is a whole number; I'm the smallest obtuse angle. _____

12. My measure is a whole number; I'm the largest acute angle. _____

NAME _____   DATE _____

3-2   QUILTING LINES

The quilts of Colonial Americans had a precise pattern based on mathematics. Find all of the parallel and perpendicular line segments in this original quilt. Write your answers on the back of this sheet.

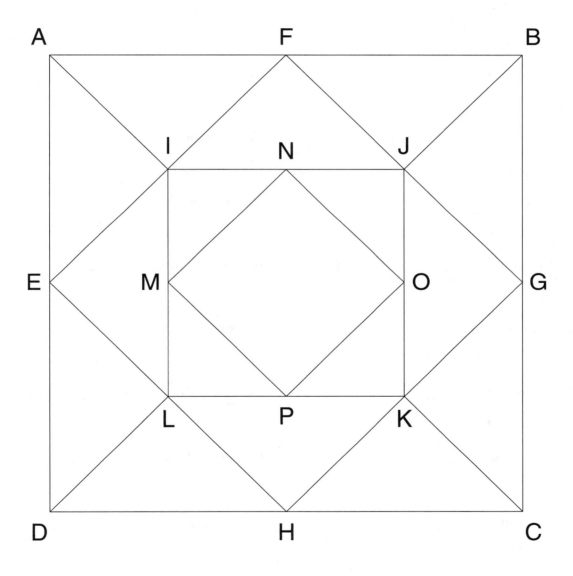

NAME _____ DATE _____

3-3 COUNTING SIDES

Write the number of sides of each polygon below. The number of sides ranges from three to twenty.

1. enneadecagon _____

2. pentagon _____

3. dodecagon _____

4. decagon _____

5. hexadecagon _____

6. triangle _____

7. nonagon _____

8. icosagon _____

9. hexagon _____

10. heptadecagon _____

11. hendecagon _____

12. quadrilateral _____

13. octadecagon _____

14. triskaidecagon _____

15. heptagon _____

16. pentadecagon _____

17. octagon _____

18. tetrakaidecagon _____

NAME _____   DATE _____

3-4 SOMETIMES IT'S RIGHT!

Find the missing angle of each triangle. Classify each triangle as acute, obtuse, or right, then note a common characteristic of the missing angles.

1.

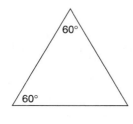

_____

2.

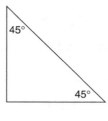

_____

3.

_____

4.

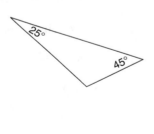

_____

5.

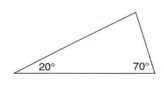

_____

6.

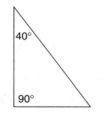

_____

7.

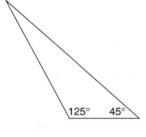

_____

8.

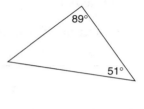

_____

9.

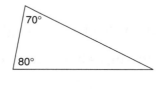

_____

Common characteristic: _____

NAME _____ DATE _____

3-5 FIND THE RIGHT WORD

Use the words from the Answer Bank to complete the story about Sylvia and triangles. A word can be used only once, and not all words will be used.

Sylvia's geometry teacher announced that the class would have a quiz on triangles the next day. That night Sylvia began to study.

She noted that there are three ways to classify triangles according to the lengths of their sides. _____ triangles have three congruent sides, isosceles triangles have at least _____ congruent sides, and _____ triangles have no congruent sides. She also noted that _____ equilateral triangles are isosceles.

To classify triangles according to the measure of their angles, she realized that right triangles have one right angle and one pair of _____ angles because the sum of these two acute angles equals 90 degrees. She also noted that an acute triangle has _____ acute angles, and that an obtuse triangle has one _____ angle and two _____ angles. Sylvia remembered that an equiangular triangle is a special type of acute triangle, because each angle measures _____ degrees. She recalled that some _____ triangles can have a right angle but that _____ equilateral triangle is an obtuse triangle. Finally, she noted that the sum of the _____ angles of every triangle is 180 degrees.

The next day Sylvia felt confident when taking the quiz.

Copyright © 2004 by Judith A. Muschla and Gary Robert Muschla

Answer Bank

no	equilateral	exterior	isosceles	thirty	some	complementary
three	sixty	interior	two	all	obtuse	scalene	right
		supplementary		acute		

NAME _____   DATE _____

3-6   WHAT'S MY LINE?

Consider the diagram below. Follow the instructions to label the points and draw the lines that are described. Fill in any blanks with the correct term.

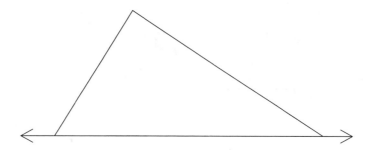

1. Label the vertices of the base of the triangle A and B. The vertex of $\angle A$ is to the left of the vertex of $\angle B$.

2. Label the other angle of the triangle $\angle C$.

3. Find the midpoint of $\overline{AB}$ and label it D.

4. Draw a line segment perpendicular to $\overline{AB}$ and name the point on the segment Point E.
    $\overline{ED}$ is the _____ of $\overline{AB}$.

5. Draw a line segment from C to D. $\overline{CD}$ is a _____ of $\triangle ACB$.

6. Draw a line segment from A to a point on $\overline{CB}$ so that this segment and $\overline{CB}$ form a right angle with Point F as a vertex. $\overline{AF}$ is an _____ of $\triangle ABC$.

7. Draw a ray from $\angle B$ to $\overline{AC}$ so that this ray bisects $\angle B$ and intersects $\overline{AC}$ at G. $\overline{BG}$ is an _____ of $\triangle ABC$.

NAME _____ DATE _____

3-7 ANGLES AND MEASURES

In the diagram below $l_1 \parallel l_2 \parallel \overleftrightarrow{AB}$ and $l_3 \parallel l_4$. l_5 intersects all lines and $\overleftrightarrow{AB}$ as shown. If the $m\angle 2 = 70°$ and $m\angle 15 = 150°$, find the measures of each of the other angles.

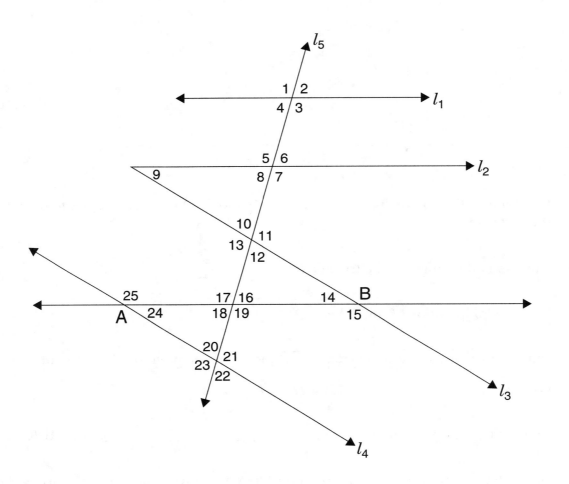

NAME _____ DATE _____

3-8   A QUADRILATERAL BY ANY OTHER NAME

Write all the names for each of the quadrilaterals below. Use the names from the Answer Bank.

1.

_____

_____

_____

_____

_____

2.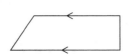

_____

_____

_____

_____

_____

3.

_____

_____

_____

_____

_____

4.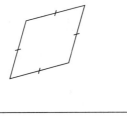

_____

_____

_____

_____

5.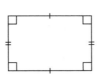

_____

_____

_____

_____

6.

_____

_____

_____

_____

Answer Bank

quadrilateral   square   rhombus   parallelogram   rectangle   trapezoid

3-9   WHAT'S THE MEASURE?

Find the measures of the missing angles. Write them in the figures.

1.
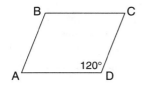

parallelogram

2.

square

3.
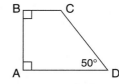

trapezoid

4.
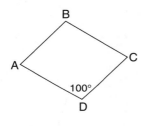

rhombus

5.
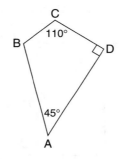

quadrilateral

6.
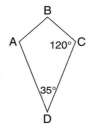

kite

7.
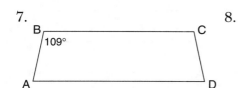

isosceles trapezoid

8.

rectangle

9.
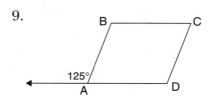

parallelogram

NAME _____ DATE _____

3–10   A POLYGON WORD FIND

Thirty-one words associated with polygons are hidden in this word find. They may be written across, down, diagonally, from left to right, right to left, or even from bottom to top. Find all thirty-one terms.

```
G  E  L  G  N  A  T  C  E  R  P  A  R  A  L  L  E  L  M
P  A  R  A  L  L  E  L  O  G  R  A  M  E  V  I  N  E  P
P  E  R  P  E  N  D  I  C  U  L  A  R  T  B  N  A  P  E
S  N  A  E  D  I  S  E  G  M  E  N  T  I  Z  E  L  X  R
Q  E  Y  N  O  G  A  T  C  O  S  A  R  K  G  O  P  E  I
U  L  E  E  R  G  E  D  H  B  W  E  I  J  C  H  T  T  M
A  A  D  E  Q  U  I  L  A  T  E  R  A  L  V  U  T  R  E
R  C  T  O  R  H  O  M  B  U  S  A  N  Q  C  S  N  E  T
E  S  P  O  L  Y  G  O  N  S  N  O  G  A  X  E  H  V  E
Q  U  A  D  R  I  L  A  T  E  R  A  L  A  N  G  L  E  R
P  E  N  T  A  G  O  N  F  S  E  L  E  C  S  O  S  I  K
T  R  A  P  E  Z  O  I  D  B  T  H  G  I  A  R  T  S  Y
```

NAME _____   DATE _____

3-11   ALWAYS, SOMETIMES, NEVER

Complete each statement with ALWAYS if the statement is always true, SOMETIMES if the statement may be true, and NEVER if the statement is never true.

1. A right angle _____ has a measure of 90°.

2. Two acute angles are _____ complementary.

3. Two obtuse angles are _____ supplementary.

4. A straight angle is _____ the same as a line.

5. Three angles of a triangle are _____ congruent.

6. An obtuse triangle _____ has an acute angle.

7. An obtuse triangle _____ has a right angle.

8. Two right angles are _____ complementary.

9. A square _____ has four right angles.

10. A rhombus _____ has four right angles.

11. Two squares are _____ congruent.

12. A right angle and an obtuse angle are _____ supplementary.

13. Two acute angles are _____ congruent.

14. A rectangle is _____ a square.

15. Opposite sides of a quadrilateral are _____ congruent.

NAME _____ DATE _____

3–12 DIFFERENT AND YET THE SAME

All of the angles and figures in each row have a common characteristic. Identify these characteristics.

1.   70°   20°   28°   62°   45°   45°

2.   15°   85°   29°

3. 15°   75°   90°   28°   65°   87°   126°   31°   23°

4.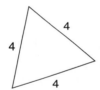

5.

6.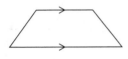

NAME _____ DATE _____

3-12 DIFFERENT AND YET THE SAME (continued)

7.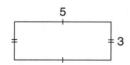

8.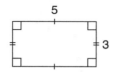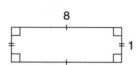

9.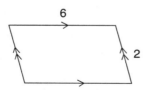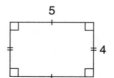

10.

3–13   WHAT'S THE RELATIONSHIP?

Four angles are related in the following ways:

- $m\angle A$ is three times the $m\angle B$.
- $m\angle C$ is 15 more than the $m\angle B$.
- $m\angle D$ is 27 more than $2m\angle B$.

Find the measure of each angle and the $m\angle B$ so that each of the following relationships is true:

1. $\angle A \approx \angle D$

2. $\angle C$ is a right angle.

3. $\angle A$ and $\angle C$ are complementary.

4. $\angle A$ and $\angle B$ are supplementary.

5. $\angle A$, $\angle B$, and $\angle D$ form an acute triangle.

6. $\angle A$, $\angle B$, $\angle C$, and $\angle D$ form a quadrilateral.

7. Two angles congruent to $\angle C$ are the base angles of an isosceles triangle. $\angle D$ is the vertex angle.

8. Four angles congruent to $\angle A$ form a rectangle.

NAME _____ DATE _____

3-14 ALL, SOME, OR NO

Fill in the blanks with ALL, SOME, or NO to make each statement true.

1. _____ similar figures have the same shape.

2. _____ similar figures have the same size.

3. _____ right triangles are congruent.

4. _____ equilateral triangles are congruent.

5. _____ equilateral triangles are similar to right triangles.

6. _____ equilateral triangles are similar to acute triangles.

7. _____ squares are similar.

8. _____ rectangles that have the same area are congruent.

9. _____ angles of a rectangle and the angles of a similar rectangle are 90°.

10. _____ circles that have the same radii are congruent.

NAME _____ DATE _____

3-15 FINDING THE PROOF

Consider the information for each pair of triangles below. Provide the necessary information to prove them congruent according to the given theorems.

I. $\triangle ABC$ and $\triangle DEF$ are drawn below. $\angle A \cong \angle D$. Supply the necessary information to show $\triangle ABC \cong \triangle DEF$ by . . .

1. SSS   2. SAS

3. AAS   4. ASA

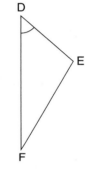

II. $\triangle GHI$ and $\triangle KLJ$ are right triangles. $\angle G$ and $\angle K$ are right angles. Supply the necessary information to show $\triangle GHI \cong \triangle KLJ$ by . . .

5. HL   6. SAS

7. AAS   8. ASA

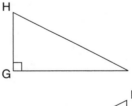

III. Consider $\triangle MNO$ and $\triangle QPO$. $\overline{MN} \parallel \overline{QP}$. Supply the necessary information to prove $\triangle MNO \cong \triangle QPO$ by . . .

9. SSS   10. SAS

11. AAS   12. ASA

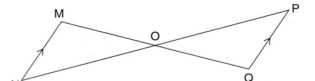

NAME _____   DATE _____

3-16 FINDING RIGHT TRIANGLES

Of the ten sets of sides of triangles below, five form right triangles. Identify each of these triangles. Then change the length of a leg of each of the other triangles so that the triangle will be a right triangle. Note: All lengths of legs should be whole numbers.

1. 3   4   5   _____

2. 5   12   13   _____

3. 9   33   41   _____

4. 11   35   37   _____

5. 12   16   20   _____

6. 15   37   39   _____

7. 20   21   29   _____

8. 20   89   101 _____

9. 57   63   87   _____

10. 468   595   757 _____

NAME _____ DATE _____

3-17 FIGURE THIS

Each set of numbers below represents the lengths of the legs of triangles. Each could either be a $45° - 45° - 90°$ triangle or a $30° - 60° - 90°$ triangle. One length in each set is missing. Find the missing length and identify the triangle.

1. 15 _____ $15\sqrt{2}$ _____

2. 1 $\sqrt{3}$ _____ _____

3. $\sqrt{5}$ $\sqrt{15}$ _____ _____

4. $5\sqrt{2}$ _____ 10 _____

5. _____ $\sqrt{3}$ $\sqrt{6}$ _____

6. _____ $3\sqrt{2}$ $2\sqrt{6}$ _____

7. $3\sqrt{2}$ $3\sqrt{6}$ _____ _____

8. _____ $2\sqrt{2}$ 4 _____

9. _____ $30\sqrt{5}$ $20\sqrt{15}$ _____

10. $\sqrt{10}$ _____ $2\sqrt{5}$ _____

NAME _____ DATE _____

3-18 PICTURE THIS

Several types of geometric figures have a different number of lines of symmetry. Draw the figures described below. Use the back of this sheet if you need more space.

1. Draw an angle that has one line of symmetry.

2. Draw two intersecting lines that have two lines of symmetry.

3. Draw a triangle that has one line of symmetry.

4. Draw a triangle that has three lines of symmetry.

5. Draw a quadrilateral with no lines of symmetry.

6. Draw a quadrilateral with one line of symmetry.

7. Draw a quadrilateral with two lines of symmetry.

8. Draw a quadrilateral with four lines of symmetry.

9. Draw a pentagon with one line of symmetry.

10. Draw a pentagon with five lines of symmetry.

NAME _____ DATE _____

3-19 SPINNING AROUND

Identify which figures below have line symmetry, rotational symmetry, both line and rotational symmetry, or neither. Write your answer under each figure.

1.

2.

3.

4.

5.

6.

7.

8.

9.

10.

11.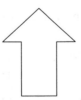

12.

NAME _____ DATE _____

3-20 DON'T GO IN CIRCLES!

Use the clues to unscramble each term related to circles.

1. **rac:** a homophone for Noah's boat _____

2. **tencer:** in the middle _____

3. **cohrd:** a combination of musical notes _____

4. **sciemirelc:** half of a circle _____

5. **ip:** a homophone for a type of dessert _____

6. **riccle rapgh:** a method for showing data _____

7. **gederes:** 360 of these equal a circle _____

8. **idarus:** half of the longest chord _____

9. **ccronentic rilecsc:** dartboard and bull's-eye _____

10. **hewel:** a prehistoric invention _____

11. **rhespe:** globe _____

12. **etierdam:** through the middle _____

13. **rsing:** usually worn on the fingers _____

14. **cpomact scid:** usually referred to by two letters _____

15. **cefcerimucern:** a little more than six times the radius _____

NAME _____ DATE _____

3–21   A CIRCLE WORD FIND

Eighteen words about circles are hidden in the word find. They may be written across, down, from left to right or right to left, or even from bottom to top. Find all eighteen.

```
A  R  C  H  O  R  D  I  C  I  R  T  N  E  C  N  O  C
J  D  E  L  V  A  W  M  A  D  U  T  A  N  G  E  N  T
Y  T  N  P  K  D  I  A  M  E  T  E  R  W  E  N  C  S
J  S  T  I  I  D  A  R  G  T  E  C  I  R  C  L  E
X  F  E  W  U  U  O  B  J  R  A  I  L  L  W  V  S  C
T  R  R  U  D  S  W  U  N  E  E  L  E  Y  J  H  W  A
C  M  C  I  R  C  U  M  F  E  R  E  N  C  E  Q  O  N
D  I  N  S  C  R  I  B  E  D  A  N  G  L  E  I  Y  T
S  E  M  I  C  I  R  C  L  E  B  H  T  A  P  R  I  V
C  E  N  T  R  A  L  A  N  G  L  E  H  W  E  P  O  R
```

NAME _____ DATE _____

3–22 COMPLETE THE CIRCLE

Use the diagram to answer each question. Any information you supply can be used in any following question. All answers are in the Answer Bank.

1. All points on the circle are the same distance from *O*. *O* is the _____.

2. $\overline{OA}$ and $\overline{OB}$ are _____.

3. $\triangle OAB$ is a(n) _____ triangle.

4. $m\widehat{AB}$ = _____ °

5. $m\angle OAB$ = _____ °

6. $\overline{CB}$ is the _____.

7. $\overline{AB}$ is a(n) _____.

8. $m\angle AOC$ = _____ °

9. $\widehat{CB}$ is a(n) _____.

10. $\overleftrightarrow{AB}$ is a(n) _____.

11. $m\angle CAB$ = _____ °

12. $\triangle CAB$ is a(n) _____.

13. $\widehat{AB}$ is a(n) _____ arc.

14. $\widehat{ABC}$ is a(n) _____ arc.

15. $\overleftrightarrow{CD}$ is a(n) _____.

16. $\angle DCO$ is a(n) _____ angle.

17. $\angle ACE$ and $\angle ABE$ are _____ angles.

18. $\angle CBE$ is a(n) _____ angle.

19. $\angle BCE$ and $\angle CBE$ are _____ angles.

20. *D* is in the _____ of the circle.

$m\angle AOB = 50°$

Answer Bank

center	exterior	complementary	diameter	right	supplementary
chord	major	isosceles	90	minor	50	secant line	130
radii	acute	65	tangent line	right triangle	semicircle

NAME _____ DATE _____

3–23   A CIRCULAR CHAIN

Find the value of the indicated variable in each diagram. Then use the value that you found to determine the value of the variable in the next diagram. You will have finished the chain when you find the value of *b*. (The diagrams are not drawn to scale. *O* is the center of each circle.)

1.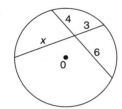

2.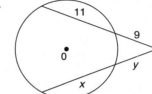

3.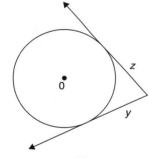

4.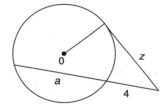

5.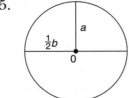

NAME _____ DATE _____

3–24 3-D WORD SCRAMBLE

Each scrambled word deals, in some way, with a three-dimensional figure. Use the clues to help you unscramble these words.

1. **buce:** Think about ice. _____

2. **ephers:** A planet. _____

3. **noce:** Ice cream. _____

4. **abes:** Used in a baseball game. _____

5. **tevrex:** All angles have one of these. _____

6. **ycinledr:** Container for canned goods. _____

7. **diyampr:** May be found in Egypt. _____

8. **acfe:** We all have one. _____

9. **sripm:** There are two types of these. _____

10. **cied:** Used in some board games. _____

11. **dege:** Faces meet here. _____

12. **riccle:** A base of a cylinder. _____

13. **ubet:** Helps children stay afloat. _____

14. **ados nac:** A great example of a cylinder. _____

15. **ctarengel:** A face of a rectangular prism. _____

16. **utialted:** Another name for height. _____

Copyright © 2004 by Judith A. Muschla and Gary Robert Muschla

NAME _____ DATE _____

3–25 FINDING 3-D FIGURES

Use the clues to identify a three-dimensional figure or part of a three-dimensional figure.

1. I have six congruent faces. _____

2. My two bases are circles. _____

3. I have six rectangular faces. _____

4. I have a circular base and a vertex that is not in the same plane as my base.
    _____

5. I am the chord that contains the center of a sphere. _____

6. I am formed by the intersection of two faces. _____

7. I am the plural of polyhedron. _____

8. I am half of a sphere. _____

9. I am a two-dimensional representation of all of the faces of a polyhedron.
    _____

10. My faces are all congruent regular polygons. _____

11. My base is a polygon and my lateral faces are triangles with a common vertex.
    _____

12. I am the point where three or more edges of a polyhedron meet.
    _____

NAME _____ DATE _____

3-26 A GREAT SWISS MATHEMATICIAN

Leonhard Euler proved that the sum of the number of faces and vertices is two more than the number of edges of a polyhedron. Use Euler's formula to complete the chart below.

		Faces	Vertices	Edges
1.	**Regular tetrahedron**	4	4	
2.	**Cube**		8	12
3.	**Regular octahedron**	8	6	
4.	**Regular dodecahedron**		20	30
5.	**Regular icosahedron**	20		30
6.	**Soccer ball**	32		90
7.	**Pyramid**	5		8
8.	**Hexagonal prism**		12	18
9.	**Triangular prism**	5		9
10.	**Pentagonal pyramid**		6	10

Section 4

MEASUREMENT

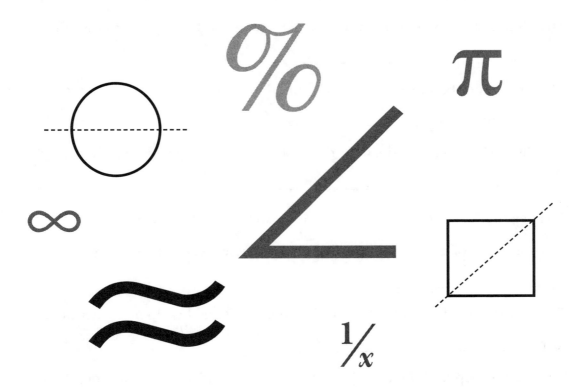

NAME _____ DATE _____

4-1   GOING TO GREAT LENGTHS

Some measures are so common that it is hard to recognize them when they are expressed in different units. Express each of the following measures as indicated.

1. The dimensions of a note card are $\frac{1}{3}$ foot by $\frac{1}{2}$ foot. Express these dimensions in inches.

   _____

2. The height of a table is one yard. Express this height in inches. _____

3. The diameter of a quarter is $\frac{1}{36}$ yard. Express this diameter in inches. _____

4. The dimensions of a round cake pan are $\frac{3}{4}$ foot in diameter by $\frac{1}{6}$ foot high. Express these dimensions in inches. _____

5. The height of a short woman is 58 inches. Express this height in feet. _____

6. The distance from New York City to Miami by car is 7,011,840 feet. Express this distance in miles. _____

7. The air distance between New York City and Miami is 1,921,920 yards. Express this distance in miles. _____

8. The dimensions of a very small room are 60 inches by 72 inches. Express these dimensions in feet. _____

9. The height of an oak tree is $23\frac{1}{3}$ yards. Express this height in feet. _____

10. One-third foot of heavy snow equals $\frac{1}{12}$ foot of water. Express these amounts in inches.

    _____

11. The average elevation of land on the Earth is 24,672 inches. Express this elevation in feet. _____

12. The average depth of the Earth's oceans is 4,012.8 yards. Express this depth in miles.

    _____

NAME _____ DATE _____

4-2 THE LONG AND SHORT OF IT

The lengths, heights, and distances of common items below are measured in metric units. However, the unit is not given. Provide the correct unit for each measurement. You may need to do some research to complete this activity.

1. The length of a sheet of notebook paper = 2.67 _____

2. The dimensions of a note card = 77 _____ by

    126 _____

3. The width of a postage stamp = 2.3 _____

4. The length of a twelve-inch ruler = 305 _____

5. The length of a pen = 1.42 _____

6. The length of a meter stick = 1,000 _____

7. The length of a yard stick = 0.91 _____

8. The height of a quart of milk = 24.5 _____

9. The diagonal of a TV screen = 48.26 _____

10. The length of a dollar bill = 155.58 _____

11. The width of a nickel = 2.22 _____

12. The height of a desk = 0.733 _____

13. The air distance between San Francisco and Washington, D.C. =

    3,931.62 _____

14. The air distance between London and Lisbon =

    1,585.85 _____

15. The length of the Nile River = 6,697.6 _____

16. The height of Mount Everest = 8,848.03 _____

NAME _____   DATE _____

4–3 GOING THE DISTANCE

Use a ruler with customary and metric units to find the lengths of the given segments in the figure. Then complete the sentences below.

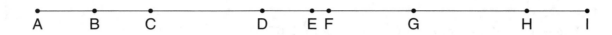

1. $AB =$ _____ centimeters

2. $AC =$ _____ inches

3. $CE =$ _____ inches

4. $EF =$ _____ millimeters

5. $CH =$ _____ centimeters

6. $BD =$ _____ millimeters

7. $BG =$ _____ inches

8. $AE =$ _____ feet

9. $BH =$ _____ decimeters

10. $HI =$ _____ inches

F is the midpoint of _____ and _____. E is the midpoint of _____.

NAME _____ DATE _____

4–4 NOT JUST FOR COOKING

Use the information below to complete the chart.

$\frac{1}{16}$ cup = 1 tablespoon	1 cup = 8 fluid ounces
$\frac{1}{16}$ cup = 3 teaspoons	1 quart = 2 pints
1 cup = $\frac{1}{2}$ pint	1 gallon = 4 quarts

1. $\frac{1}{8}$ cup = _____ tablespoons

2. $\frac{1}{4}$ cup = _____ tablespoons

3. $\frac{1}{2}$ cup = _____ tablespoons

4. 1 cup = _____ tablespoons

5. 1 cup = _____ teaspoons

6. 1 pint = _____ cups

7. 1 pint = _____ fluid ounces

8. 1 quart = _____ cups

9. 1 quart = _____ fluid ounces

10. 1 gallon = _____ pints

11. 1 gallon = _____ cups

12. 1 gallon = _____ fluid ounces

NAME _____ DATE _____

4–5 ODD MEASURE OUT

Of the three measures in each set, two are equal. Circle the one that is NOT equal to the other two.

1. 1.5 feet   0.5 yard   24 inches

2. 2 quarts   6 cups   a half gallon

3. 12 ounces   0.5 pounds $\frac{3}{4}$ pound

4. 100 yards   300 feet   0.1 mile

5. 18 fluid ounces   2 pints   4 cups

6. 15 inches   1.3 feet $1\frac{1}{4}$ feet

7. 0.75 gallons   6 pints   20 fluid ounces

8. 500 pounds   1,000 pounds   0.5 ton

9. 1 pint $\frac{1}{2}$ quart   4 cups

10. 2.5 pounds   40 ounces   0.25 pounds

11. 0.5 pints   4 fluid ounces   1 cup

12. $\frac{1}{5}$ mile   1,320 feet   0.25 mile

4–6   GETTING TO THE BASICS

The basic units in the metric system, or Système International (SI), are scrambled below. Use the clues to unscramble the metric terms.

1. **velink:** temperature   _____

2. **dnosec:** time   _____

3. **mereap:** electric current   _____

4. **elom:** amount of a substance   _____

5. **temer:** length   _____

6. **amgr:** mass   _____

7. **daceanl:** luminous intensity   _____

NAME _____ DATE _____

4–7 EQUAL OR NOT EQUAL

Each of the three measures in each set should be equivalent. Some, however, are not. Circle the number of the problem that has unequal measures, and correct the measurement that is incorrect.

1.	1 km	100 m	100,000 cm
2.	15 dm	1.5 m	150 cm
3.	1.5 kg	1,500 gr	150,000 dg
4.	200 mL	0.2 L	2 dL
5.	15.5 hg	1,550 g	155,500 cg
6.	15 mm	1.5 cm	0.15 m
7.	12 cm	1.2 mm	0.12 m
8.	200 g	0.2 kg	20,000 cg
9.	35 L	0.35 cL	3.5 mL
10.	0.98 daL	9.8 L	980 cL

Corrections:

_____

_____

_____

_____

_____

_____

_____

NAME _____   DATE _____

4–8   IT'S ABOUT TIME

Use the information below to write questions that have the given answers.

- Susan gets paid $6.50 an hour for working forty hours or less per week. Any hours more than forty she works are considered to be overtime.
- Susan gets paid time and a half for each hour of overtime she works.
- If Susan works an eight-hour day, she takes a half hour for lunch. She does not get paid for lunch, but she does get paid for two fifteen-minute breaks.
- It takes Susan twenty minutes to drive to work if she starts work before 11:00 A.M.
- If Susan leaves work after 5:00 P.M. on a weekday, it takes her thirty-five minutes to drive home.
- If she travels between 11:00 A.M. and 5:00 P.M., her ride takes only twenty-five minutes.

<table>
<tr><td colspan="3" align="center">Answers for Problems</td></tr>
<tr><td>1. 8 hours</td><td>2. 8:40 A.M.</td><td>3. $260</td></tr>
<tr><td>4. 308.75</td><td>5. 11:35 A.M., 6:35 P.M.</td><td>6. $7\frac{1}{2}$ hours</td></tr>
</table>

_____

_____

_____

_____

_____

_____

_____

_____

_____

(Continue on the back of this sheet if necessary.)

NAME _____ DATE _____

4–9 NEVER ENOUGH TIME

Solve the following problems.

1. Joe works from 8:00 A.M. to 4:00 P.M. each weekday. Each day he has a half-hour, unpaid lunch break. He is paid an hourly wage and was paid $240 last week. What is his hourly

   wage? _____

2. The student council is planning a pep rally for the football team. The pep rally must be finished by 2:15, the end of the school day. The pep rally is expected to last fifty min-

   utes. What time should it begin? _____

3. Marissa has enhanced her exercise program. She wants to work out four days every week for an average of one hour and fifteen minutes each day. So far this week she has worked out three days for seventy minutes, eighty minutes, and sixty-five minutes each.

   How long must she exercise on the fourth day to reach her goal? _____

4. The cooking time required for a four to six-pound roast is three hours. If the roast is frozen, 50% more cooking time is needed. After the roast is done, it should sit twenty-five minutes before it is carved. What time should Lisa start to cook a five-pound frozen

   roast if she plans on carving it at 7:15 P.M.? _____

5. The dining room clock chimes once at one o'clock, twice at two o'clock, and so on.

   How many times will it chime between 11:55 A.M. and 12.05 A.M.? _____

6. What was the last year that was a palindrome? What year will be the next palindrome?

   _____ _____

7. A plumber charges a $50 service fee plus $35 per hour for labor. He arrived at Teri's house at 2:15 P.M. and charged $120. Assuming he did not charge her for any new

   plumbing materials, what time did he leave? _____

8. Tom gets an hourly wage for his work on a construction crew. He is paid $9 per hour and time and a half per hour for each hour he works after a forty-hour week. Last week

   he was paid $441. How many hours did he work? _____

NAME _____   DATE _____

4-10   TIMELY WORDS

Everyone knows about years, minutes, and seconds, but there are many other words that refer to time. Use the clues to unscramble these "timely" words.

1. **tgonihtfr:** 2 weeks _____

2. **ninumebi:** 2 years _____

3. **socer:** 20 years _____

4. **liniumemnl:** 1,000 years _____

5. **nualan:** once a year _____

6. **ibnualna:** twice a year _____

7. **wibeleky:** twice a week _____

8. **anemsiaunl:** twice a year _____

9. **drenuaqialn:** once every four years _____

10. **tencenianl:** 100th anniversary _____

11. **nialibtencen:** 200th anniversary _____

12. **ntecenirtialn:** 300th anniversary _____

Section 4: Measurement

NAME _____   DATE _____

4–11   CODED EQUATIONS

Each equation represents a type of measure. Decipher the measures. The first one is done for you.

1. 12 = I in a F   _____ *12 = inches in a foot* _____

2. 100 = C in a D   _____

3   90 = F between B in BB _____

4. 4 = Q in a G   _____

5. 4 = Q in a D   _____

6. 90 = D in a RA   _____

7. 20 = Y in a S   _____

8. 144 = I in a G   _____

9. 500 = S of P in a R   _____

10. X = T in RN   _____

11. 4 = S in a Y   _____

12. 24 = H in a D   _____

13. 186,282 mps = S of L   _____

14. 2R = D   _____

15. 144 = SI in a SF   _____

NAME _____   DATE _____

4–12   HOW DO YOU MEASURE UP?

Numbers that represent the relationships between two quantities are listed below. State the relationship. (Some numbers may have more than one answer.) The first one is done for you.

1. 2 _____ *2 pints = 1 quart* _____

2. 3 _____

3. 4 _____

4. 7 _____

5. 8 _____

6. 9 _____

7. 10 _____

8. 12 _____

9. 16 _____

10. 24 _____

11. 36 _____

12. 60 _____

13. 90 _____

14. 100 _____

15. 144 _____

16. 180 _____

17. 360 _____

18. 1,760 _____

19. 2,000 _____

20. 5,280 _____

NAME _____ DATE _____

4-13 TAKE YOUR MEASURE

All of the words below relate to measurement in some way. Use the clues to help you unscramble these miscellaneous measures. (You may need to consult reference sources for some!)

1. **rsogs:** 12 dozen _____

2. **cidebel:** unit of relative loudness _____

3. **tolb:** 40 yards of cloth _____

4. **arec:** 43,560 square feet _____

5. **weorsphreo:** power of engines _____

6. **mear:** paper _____

7. **perame:** electrical current _____

8. **tonk:** speed of ships _____

9. **ozend:** 12 units _____

10. **moh:** electrical resistance _____

11. **nacih:** used in surveying _____

12. **hrigy-leat:** 5,880,000,000,000 miles _____

13. **imnoasaltroc nuit:** average distance from Earth to the sun

_____

14. **rakat:** purity of gold _____

15. **oscer:** 20 units _____

16. **hnad:** height of horses _____

17. **labe:** large bundle of goods _____

18. **zerht:** electromagnetic wave frequencies _____

19. **morrabtee:** air pressure _____

20. **specar:** about 3.26 light-years _____

NAME _____ DATE _____

4–14 MATCHING TEMPERATURES

Some common temperatures are expressed in column 1. Match each with an equivalent temperature in column 2.

Column 1	**Column 2**
1. 374° F, a hot oven _____	37° C
2. 45° C, a hot bath _____	113° F
3. 23° F, a snowy day _____	212° F
4. 32° F, freezing point of water _____	44.6° F
5. 40° C, a high fever _____	190° C
6. 98.6° F, normal body temperature _____	80° C
7. 100° C, boiling point of water _____	0° C
8. 7° C, cold water _____	95° F
9. 176° F, hot soup _____	104° F
10. 35° C, a hot day _____	–5° C

NAME _____ DATE _____

4-15   A MATTER OF DEGREE

Measure each angle. Find the measure in the Answer Bank, and then place the letter of the measure in the space before the angle. Correct answers (in order) will reveal the name of an important measuring device. Not all measures will be used.

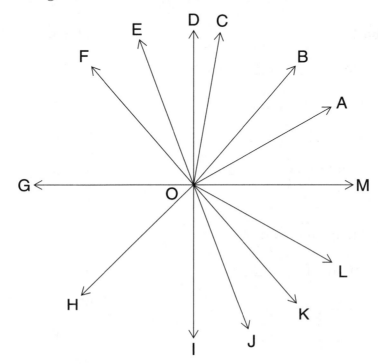

1. _____ $m\angle EOG$ = _____

2. _____ $m\angle MOB$ = _____

3. _____ $m\angle FOD$ = _____

4. _____ $m\angle BOG$ = _____

5. _____ $m\angle MOD$ = _____

6. _____ $m\angle IOK$ = _____

7. _____ $m\angle MOJ$ = _____

8. _____ $m\angle GOA$ = _____

9. _____ $m\angle MOI$ = _____

10. _____ $m\angle GOK$ = _____

11. _____ $m\angle KOI$ = _____

Answer Bank

O. 130°	**R.** 40°	**A.** 70°	**S.** 35°	**P.** 50°	**T.** 90°
U. 45°	**E.** 110°	**L.** 100°	**C.** 150°		

NAME _____   DATE _____

4–16   A SLICE OF THE CIRCLE

Angles may always be measured in degrees, but in advanced mathematics they are also measured in radians. The angles below are given in order from least to greatest, but they are not in the same increments. If the measure of the angle is expressed in degrees, find the measure in radians. If the measure of the angle is expressed in radians, find the number of degrees.

1. 30° _____

2. _____ $\dfrac{\pi}{4}$

3. 60° _____

4. _____ $\dfrac{5\pi}{12}$

5. 90° _____

6. 105° _____

7. _____ $\dfrac{2\pi}{3}$

8. _____ $\dfrac{3\pi}{4}$

9. 150° _____

10. _____ $\dfrac{11\pi}{12}$

11. _____ π

12. 210° _____

13. _____ $\dfrac{4\pi}{3}$

14. 270° _____

15. 300° _____

16. _____ 2π

NAME _____ DATE _____

4-17   FINDING THE WAY AROUND

Given the perimeters of the figures below, find the missing length(s). Use 3.14 for π.

1.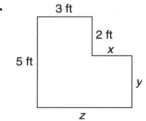

12 cm

x

120 mm

Perimeter = 42 cm

Length: _____

2.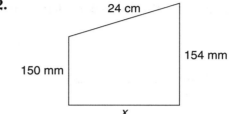

24 cm

154 mm

150 mm

x

Perimeter = 75.4 cm

Length: _____

3.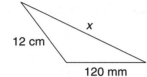

3 ft

2 ft

x

5 ft

y

z

Perimeter = 20 ft.

Lengths: _____

_____

4.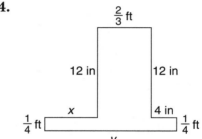

$\frac{2}{3}$ ft

12 in   12 in

x   4 in

$\frac{1}{4}$ ft $\frac{1}{4}$ ft

y

Perimeter = 66 in.

Lengths: _____

_____

5.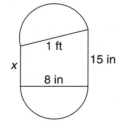

1 ft

15 in

x

8 in

Perimeter = 50.4 in.

Length: _____

6.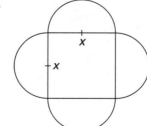

x

x

Perimeter = 157 cm

Length: _____

NAME _____ DATE _____

4–18 GOING AROUND IN "SQUARES"

A pentomino is a figure comprising five congruent squares so that the vertices of the angles "touch" and the sides coincide. The possible arrangements are shown below.

Each square has an area of 25 square inches. Circle the pentomino that has the smallest perimeter.

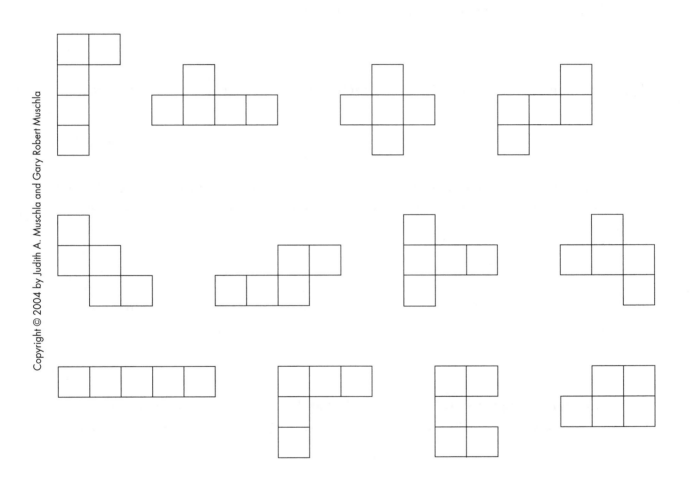

NAME _____ DATE _____

4–19 SKETCHING IT OUT

Making a drawing or diagram is a great strategy for solving some types of problems. Use this strategy to answer the questions below. Note: All of the sides in the squares and rectangles are whole numbers.

1. A square has a perimeter of 20 inches. What is the area?

2. A rectangle has an area of 36 square inches. What are its five possible perimeters?

3. A rectangle and a square have the same area. The perimeter of the rectangle is four more than the perimeter of the square. What are the dimensions of the rectangle and square?

4. A certain rectangle can be divided into three congruent squares. Each square has an area of 25 square inches. What is the perimeter of the rectangle?

5. Four congruent squares are arranged such that they form one large square. The area of this large square is 100 square units. What is the perimeter of the small squares?

6. Two congruent rectangles are arranged so that they form a square. The perimeter of each rectangle is 36 inches. What is the area and the perimeter of the large square?

NAME _____   DATE _____

4–20   DIFFERENT FIGURES, SAME AREAS

For each set of three figures, find the missing length so that the areas of the figures in the set are the same.

1. **square**

    $s = 6$

    rectangle

    $l = 9$

    $w =$ _____

    parallelogram

    $b = 12$

    $h =$ _____

2. **rectangle**

    $l = 7$

    $w = 4$

    parallelogram

    $b = 2$

    $h =$ _____

    triangle

    $h = 14$

    $b =$ _____

3. **triangle**

    $b = 15$

    $h = 4$

    rectangle

    $w = 3$

    $l =$ _____

    trapezoid

    $b_1 = 15, b_2 = 5$

    $h =$ _____

4. **rectangle**

    $l = 16$

    $h = 4$

    square

    $s =$ _____

    trapezoid

    $b_1 = 12, h = 4$

    $b_2 =$ _____

5. **trapezoid**

    $b_1 = 4, b_2 = 10$

    $h = 5$

    triangle

    $b = 7$

    $h =$ _____

    rectangle

    $l = 5$

    $w =$ _____

6. **circle**

    $r = 8$

    circle

    $d =$ _____

    quarter circle

    $r =$ _____

Section 4: Measurement

105

NAME _____ DATE _____

4-21 DRAWING GEOMETRIC FIGURES

Visualizing and drawing geometric figures is quite a skill. Using another sheet of paper, try your hand at creating these shapes.

1. Draw a square and a rectangle that have the same area but different perimeters.

2. Draw a right triangle and an acute triangle that have the same area but different perimeters.

3. Draw a scalene triangle and a right triangle that have the same area but different perimeters.

4. Draw two rectangles that have the same perimeter but different areas.

5. Draw a parallelogram and a rectangle that have the same area but different perimeters.

6. Draw two congruent triangles whose combined area is the same as the area of a square.

7. Divide a square into two congruent rectangles.

8. Divide a square into two congruent irregular figures.

9. Draw a trapezoid that can be divided into three congruent triangles.

10. Draw a rhombus that can be divided into two congruent triangles.

NAME _____   DATE _____

4–22 ALL RELATED

The vertices of rhombus *ABCD* are the midpoints of the sides of rectangle *FGHI*. Use the diagram and the given information to find the area of rhombus *ABCD*. Note: The diagram is not drawn to scale.

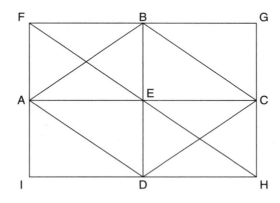

Find the area of rhombus *ABCD* if:

1. $AC = 15$, $BD = 6$ _____

2. $AE = 8$, $ED = 4$ _____

3. $AB = 5$, $BD = 8$ _____

4. $AB = 17$, $AC = 16$ _____

5. Area of $\triangle BCD = 18$ square units   _____

6. Area of $\triangle EDC = 84$ square units   _____

7. $FG = 8$, $FI = 6$ _____

8. $FH = 10$, $IH = 8$ _____

NAME _____ DATE _____

4–23 GOING FULL CIRCLE

Use the diagram to answer the questions below. You will have gone full circle when you complete all of the problems. Use 3.14 for pi.

1. Area of circle O = _____

2. Circumference of circle O = _____

3. $m\widehat{CAB}$ = _____

4. $m\angle ADC$ = _____

5. Arc length $\widehat{CB}$ = _____

6. Arc length $\widehat{AB}$ = _____

7. $m\widehat{DC}$ = _____

8. Arc length of $\widehat{DC}$ = _____

9. Area of sector BOD = _____

10. Area of sector AOD = _____

11. Area of sector AOB = _____

O is the center $AC = 10$
$m\angle COB = 45°$ $DC = OD$

12. How does the sum of your answers to problems 9 through 11 compare to your answer to problem 1?

_____

_____

_____

_____

NAME _____ DATE _____

4–24 KNOW WHAT FORMULA TO USE

Each expression on the right can be paired with a description on the left. Write the letter of the expression in the blank before its description. Some expressions may be used twice; others may not be used at all.

Description   **Expression**

1. _____ perimeter of a triangle   **A.** $\frac{1}{2}bh$

2. _____ area of a triangle   **B.** $2r$

3. _____ perimeter of a square   **C.** $2l + 2w$

4. _____ area of a square   **D.** $\frac{1}{2}\pi r^2$

5. _____ perimeter of a rectangle   **E.** $4s$

6. _____ area of a rectangle   **F.** $\frac{1}{2}h(b_1 + b_2)$

7. _____ area of a parallelogram   **G.** s^2

8. _____ area of a trapezoid   **H.** πd

9. _____ diameter of a circle   **I.** $a + b + c$

10. _____ circumference of a circle   **J.** bh

11. _____ area of a circle   **K.** πr^2

12. _____ area of a semicircle   **L.** lw

NAME _____ DATE _____

4–25 FORMULAS TO THE MAX

Several formulas for area are used in high school geometry classes throughout the world. Some of the formulas appear on this sheet. Write the letter of the formula(s) after the name of the figure to which it or they apply. All formulas on the page will be used, and some can be matched with more than one figure. Also, some figures can be matched with more than one formula. (A list of what each variable represents is included at the end of the activity.)

Figure

Formula

1. triangle _____

2. equilateral triangle _____

3. square _____

4. trapezoid _____

5. rhombus _____

6. kite _____

7. regular polygon _____

A. $A = \dfrac{s^2\sqrt{3}}{4}$

B. $A = sa$

C. $A = \dfrac{d_1^2}{2}$

D. $A = \sqrt{s(s-a)(s-b)(s-c)}$

E. $A = mh$

F. $A = \dfrac{d_1 d_2}{2}$

G. $A = \dfrac{h^2\sqrt{3}}{3}$

H. $A = \dfrac{nsa}{2}$

Variables

m = median	s = half the perimeter
h = height	n = the number of congruent sides
d_1 = a diagonal	a = the apothem
d_2 = another diagonal	a_1, a_2, a_3 = three sides

NAME _____ DATE _____

4–26   A STEP BEYOND

Complete the chart and find the missing numbers. The diagrams are not drawn to scale. The area is expressed in square units, and volume is expressed in cubic units.

	Surface Area (in Square Units)	**Volume (in Cubic Units)**
1. cube	_____	_____
2. cube	_____	125
3. cube	294	_____
4. rectangular prism	_____	_____

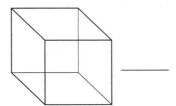

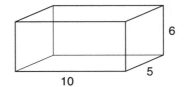

NAME _____ DATE _____

4–26 A STEP BEYOND (continued)

	Surface Area (in Square Units)	Volume (in Cubic Units)	

5. rectangular
prism

_____   *288*

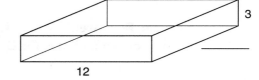

6. rectangular
prism

148   _____

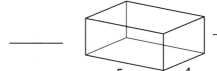

7. triangular
prism

_____   _____

8. triangular
prism

_____   *60*

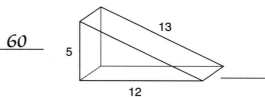

NAME _____ DATE _____

4–27 SAME AND DIFFERENT

Two of the figures in each set have the same volume or surface area. Find these figures and find the volume or surface area. The diagrams are not drawn to scale.

1. Which figures have the same volume? _____

$V =$ _____

 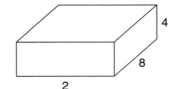 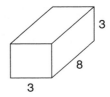

2. Which figures have the same surface area? _____

$SA =$ _____

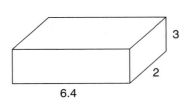 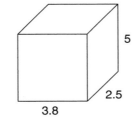 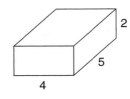

3. Which figures have the same volume? _____

$V \approx$ _____

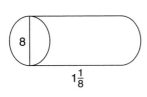 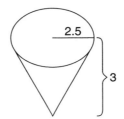 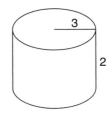

NAME _____ DATE _____

4–27 SAME AND DIFFERENT *(continued)*

4. Which figures have the same volume? _____

$V =$ _____

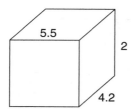 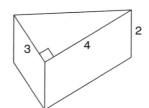 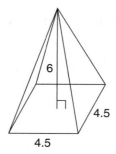

5. Which figures have the same surface area? _____

$SA \approx$ _____

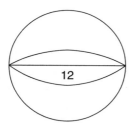 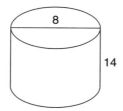 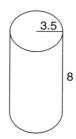

NAME _____ DATE _____

4–28 WHAT'S THE VALUE?

Find the indicated value so that the figures will have the same surface area or volume.

1. A rectangular prism has a length of 2 units and a height of 16 units. Find the width so that it has the same volume as a cube whose edge is 4 units. _____

2. The base of a triangular prism is a right triangle whose legs are 6 units and 8 units. The height is 5 units. Find the height of a triangular pyramid with the same base so that both figures will have the same volume. _____

3. A cylinder has a height of 6 units. Find the radius so that it has the same volume as a cone whose radius is 1 unit and whose height is 2 units. _____

4. A sphere has a radius of 1 unit. Find the height of a cylinder that has a radius of 1 unit so that the volumes are the same. _____

5. A cube has a side of 5 units. The base of a triangular prism is a right triangle whose legs measure 5 units and 12 units. Find the height of this prism so that both figures have the same surface area. _____

6. Find the side of a cube so that it has the same surface area as a rectangular prism whose measurements are 3 units by 4 units by 6 units. _____

7. Two triangular pyramids have square bases. One base is 6 units by 6 units and the slant height is 5 units. The other base is 8 units by 8 units. Find the slant height of the second pyramid so that both surface areas are the same. _____

8. A cone and a cylinder have the same radii. The height of the cylinder is 5 units. The slant height of the cone is 11 units. Find the radii. _____

9. A cone has a radius of 4 units and a slant height of 6 units. Find the radius of a sphere so that both surface areas are the same. _____

NAME _____ DATE _____

4-29 DOUBLE TROUBLE

Doubling a part of a geometric figure affects the area, perimeter, and circumference of plane figures, and the surface area and volume of three-dimensional figures. Find how doubling a length affects the various measures in the problems below.

1. Double the length of each side of a square. The perimeter is _____ and the

   area is _____ times the area of the original square.

2. Double the length of a rectangle. The perimeter is increased by _____ the

   original length and the area is _____ times the area of the original rectangle.

3. Double the radius of a circle. The diameter is _____, the circumference is

   _____, and the area is _____ times the area of the original circle.

4. Double each side of a right triangle. The perimeter is _____ and the area

   is _____ times the area of the original right triangle.

5. Double each edge of a cube. The volume is _____ times the volume of the original

   cube. The surface area is _____ times the surface area of the original cube.

6. Double the radius and the height of a cylinder. The volume is _____ times the
   volume of the original cylinder.

NAME _____   DATE _____

4–30 MEASURING UP

Write T for each true statement and F for each false statement. Then state a reason for your answer. (If necessary, consult a table of measurements for the values of units.) When you are done, match the true and false statements for each question with the corresponding letters in the Answer Bank to complete the statement at the end of the activity. The first problem has been calculated for you.

1. There are more inches in a mile than ounces in a ton.

    T 1 mile = 63,360 inches; 1 ton = 32,000 ounces

2. There are more minutes in a day than seconds in four hours.

    _____

3. There are more yards in five miles than feet in two and a half miles.

    _____

4. There are more square inches in a square foot than square feet in ten square yards.

    _____

5. There are more fluid ounces in a pint than pints in a gallon.

    _____

6. There are more square inches in a square yard than cubic inches in a cubic yard.

    _____

7. There are more tablespoons in a cup than fluid ounces in a gallon.

    _____

Answer Bank

1. T, b; F, t   **2.** T, e; F, a   **3.** T, a; F, r   **4.** T, l; F, r   **5.** T, e; F, h   **6.** T, a; F, y
7. T, r; F, c   **8.** T, s; F, o   **9.** T, r; F, s   **10.** T, t; F, n   **11.** T, s; F, r

4–30 MEASURING UP (continued)

8. There are more yards in half a mile than square yards in half an acre.

   _____

9. There are more inches in twenty feet than units between freezing and boiling on the Fahrenheit scale.

   _____

10. There are more fluid ounces in four gallons than acres in a square mile.

    _____

11. There are more cubic inches in a cubic foot than inches in five yards.

    _____

In the past, one inch was equal to three *b*_____ .

Section 5

ALGEBRA

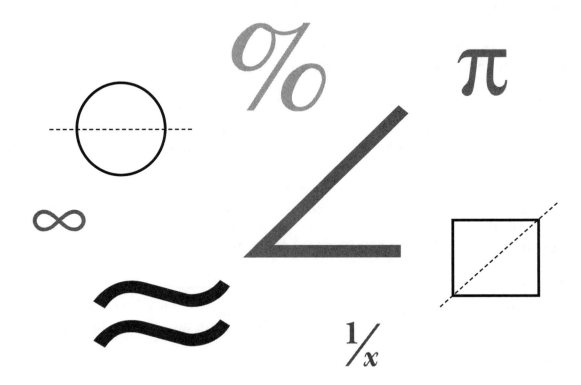

NAME_____ DATE_____

5-1 FINDING SOLUTIONS

The problems below contain variables instead of numbers. For each problem write an expression to represent the information. The first one is done for you.

1. Meg's dog, Cuddly, is a years old. Each year in a dog's life is equivalent to about b years in human years. How old is Cuddly in human years? _____$a \times b$_____

2. Sunil recently drove his car to Florida for a vacation. Before the trip, the car's odometer read a miles. After the trip it read b miles. How many miles did Sunil travel on his

    vacation? _____

3. On a trip to visit her cousin in a nearby state, Jennifer and her parents drove a miles

    in b hours. What was their average speed? _____

4. Pedro and his father belong to a bicycle club. On a recent tour the first leg was a miles, the second leg was b miles, and the third leg was c miles. How long was the tour?

    _____

5. Marissa worked a hours on Monday after school and b hours on Thursday. She was paid

    c dollars. How much did she earn per hour? _____

6. The Ryan High School basketball team enjoys excellent support from its fans. The attendance for the first five games of their season was a, b, c, d, and e. What was the aver-

    age attendance? _____

7. Carl and Luis are members of their school's track team. Along with working out with the team, they also work out on their own. On Saturday Carl ran a miles and on Sunday he ran b miles. On Saturday Luis ran c miles and on Sunday he ran d miles.

    Who ran more miles? _____

8. The High Ridge Ski Lodge has several long trails. Eagle Trail is a miles long. Wolf Trail is b miles long. Together Eagle Trail and Wolf Trail are two times as long as Big Sky

    Trail. How long is Big Sky Trail? _____

Copyright © 2004 by Judith A. Muschla and Gary Robert Muschla

NAME _____   DATE _____

5-2 ACCORDING TO THE FACTS

Use the information in the Data Bank to fill in the blanks that follow.

1. Sue is 39 years old. Jon's age is _____.
2. Carl is 54 years old. Mike's age is _____.
3. Margaret is 42 years old. Dee's age is _____.
4. Ann is 58 years old. Silvia's age is _____.
5. I have 23 nickels. I have _____ dimes.
6. The width is 10 units. The length is _____ units.
7. Bob is 17 years old. Carlos's age is _____.
8. Bev weighs 97 pounds. Tracy weighs _____ pounds.
9. Carol has 13 hats. Ann has _____ hats. Bev has _____ hats.
10. Side$_3$ is 21 units. Side$_1$ is _____ units. Side$_2$ is _____ units.
11. I have 29 dimes. I have _____ pennies and _____ nickels.
12. Car 1 costs $15,000. Car 2 costs _____ and car 3 costs _____.
13. Lou ran for 20 seconds. Rich ran the same distance in _____ seconds. Bob ran the same distance in _____ seconds.
14. Sue weighs 145 pounds. Mary weighs _____ pounds; Phil weighs _____ pounds.
15. Marco is 29 years old. Juan is _____ years old.
16. Smith High won 15 games. Jones High won _____ games. Eagle High won _____ games.
17. I have 23 pennies. I have _____ dimes, _____ nickels, and _____ quarters.
18. Phil has 23 dollars. Carl has _____ dollars, Bill has _____ dollars, and Tracy has _____ dollars.

Data Bank

1. Jon is six years older than Sue.
2. Carl is twice Mike's age.
3. Dee is three years younger than Margaret.
4. Silvia is half Ann's age.
5. I have six fewer nickels than dimes.
6. The length is three times the width.
7. Carlos is two years older than twice Bob's age.
8. Tracy is 205 pounds lighter than three times Bev's weight.
9. Ann has seven more hats than Carol. Bev has two fewer hats than Carol.
10. Side$_1$ of a triangle is two more than Side$_3$. Side$_2$ of a triangle is three more than Side$_1$.
11. I have six more pennies than dimes. I have two fewer nickels than dimes.
12. Car 1 costs $4,000 more than car 3. Car 2 costs $1,000 more than car 1.
13. Rich runs twice as fast as Lou. Bob runs six seconds slower than Rich.
14. Sue weighs 20 pounds less than Mary. Phil weighs 70 pounds more than Mary.
15. Juan is five years younger than twice Marco's age.
16. Smith High won three more games than Jones High. Eagle High won two more games than both Smith High and Jones High.
17. I have seven more nickels than pennies. I have five fewer dimes than nickels. I have twice as many quarters as nickels.
18. Carl has six dollars less than three times the amount of money Phil has. Bill has eight dollars more than Carl. Tracy has the same amount of money as the sum of Phil and Bill.

NAME _____ DATE _____

5-3   A SWEET TIME LINE

Many favorite candies have withstood the taste test for more than a century. A list of favorites and the year they were first sold follows. Place each at the appropriate point on the time line.

Almond Joy, 1947   M&M's, 1920

Baby Ruth, 1921   Milky Way, 1923

Cracker Jack, 1896   Reese's Pieces, 1978

Hershey's Bar, 1894   Snickers, 1930

Hershey's Kisses, 1907   3 Musketeers, 1932

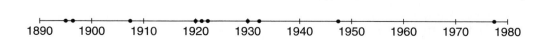

1890 1900 1910 1920 1930 1940 1950 1960 1970 1980

NAME _____ DATE _____

5-4 A PLACE FOR EVERYTHING

Follow the directions to place each coordinate at its correct point on the number line.

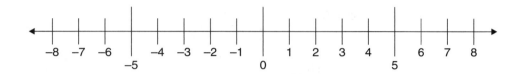

1. 0 is the coordinate of *O*.

2. *A* is 5 units to the right of *O*.

3. *H* is 2 units from *A* and 3 units from *O*.

4. *I* is 2 units to the left of *O*.

5. *B* is 5 units from *I*.

6. *O* is the midpoint of $\overline{IF}$.

7. *C* is the midpoint of $\overline{HA}$.

8. *K* is 5 units from *H*.

9. *M* is the same distance from zero as *A* is.

10. *L* is 1 unit from *F*.

11. *N* is paired with the opposite of the value that *H* is paired with.

12. *R* is 1 unit from *N*.

13. *S* is the largest negative integer.

14. *T* is 1 unit to the left of *B*; *X* is 1 unit to the right of *B*.

15. The distance from *F* to *E* is 5 units.

16. *Z* is between *A* and *E*.

NAME _____ DATE _____

5–5   FINDING EQUAL EXPRESSIONS

Place an addition or subtraction symbol in each space so that the expression on the left equals the expression on the right.

1. 3 ___ –3 = 5 ___ 1

2. –2 ___ 6 = –10 ___ 2

3. –7 ___ 3 = –2 ___ –2

4. –8 ___ –2 = 5 ___ 11

5. –15 ___ –2 = 20 ___ –37

6. –3 ___ 4 ___ –5 = –6 ___ –6

7. –9 ___ –3 ___ –10 = 12 ___ –8

8. –10 ___ –2 ___ 13 = –8 ___ –6 ___ 7

9. –2 ___ –3 ___ 5 = –2 ___ 4 ___ 8 ___ 10

10. –3 ___ 8 ___ –4 = 7 ___ 1 ___ 3

11. –2 ___ 3 ___ –5 = 8 ___ –2 ___ 4

12. –13 ___ –3 ___ –6 = 8 ___ –5 ___ –10 ___ –3

NAME _____   DATE _____

5-6 COUNTING DOWN

Write the expression after its answer.

	Answers	**Expressions**
1.	$10 = $ _____	$0 \div (-10)$
2.	$9 = $ _____	$-20 \div (-4)$
3.	$8 = $ _____	$-26 \div 13$
4.	$7 = $ _____	-2×2
5.	$6 = $ _____	$-5 \times (-2)$
6.	$5 = $ _____	$-36 \div 4$
7.	$4 = $ _____	$9 \div 3$
8.	$3 = $ _____	-3×2
9.	$2 = $ _____	$-3 \times (-3)$
10.	$1 = $ _____	$50 \div (-5)$
11.	$0 = $ _____	$44 \div 22$
12.	$-1 = $ _____	-4×2
13.	$-2 = $ _____	$-16 \div (-2)$
14.	$-3 = $ _____	$7 \times (-1)$
15.	$-4 = $ _____	$-28 \div (-7)$
16.	$-5 = $ _____	$-35 \div 7$
17.	$-6 = $ _____	$-18 \div (-18)$
18.	$-7 = $ _____	$-49 \div (-7)$
19.	$-8 = $ _____	-1×3
20.	$-9 = $ _____	$-3 \times (-2)$
21.	$-10 = $ _____	$8 \div (-8)$

NAME _____ DATE _____

5-7 FINDING THE LARGEST AND SMALLEST

Use the following integers to write an equation showing the two integers that will give the result stated in each problem:

−3   9   8   −6

1. The largest sum: _____

2. The largest difference: _____

3. The largest product: _____

4. The largest quotient: _____

5. The smallest sum: _____

6. The smallest difference: _____

7. The smallest product: _____

8. The smallest quotient: _____

Write the sum of your answers: _____.
(If the sum is equal to negative five squared, your math is probably correct.)

NAME _____ DATE _____

5-8 INTEGER FACTS

Complete each sentence with "always," "sometimes," or "never" to make the sentence true.

1. A positive integer is _____ greater than a negative integer.

2. The sum of two positive numbers is _____ positive.

3. The sum of two negative numbers is _____ positive.

4. The sum of a number and its opposite _____ equals zero.

5. The absolute value of a positive number plus the absolute value of the opposite of the number _____ equals zero.

6. The sum of two integers is _____ zero.

7. The sum of a positive integer and a negative integer is _____ a negative integer.

8. The product of two negative integers is _____ negative.

9. The product of a positive integer and its opposite is _____ zero.

10. The product of two negative integers is _____ less than the product of two positive integers.

11. The product of three negative integers is _____ negative.

12. If you have completed the previous sentences correctly, three of your answers were

    " _____ ."

NAME _____ DATE _____

5-9 PARENTHESES, PLEASE

A set of parentheses is missing from each equation. Rewrite the equations with the necessary parentheses to make the equations true.

1. $8 - 4 + (-3) = 7$ _____

2. $3 \times (-4) + 2 = -6$ _____

3. $18 \div (-11) + 2 = -2$ _____

4. $-9 \times 4 \div (-1) - 2 = 12$ _____

5. $-3 + 5 \div (-2) = -1$ _____

6. $-8 \div 4 - 2 \times 6 = -24$ _____

7. $32 - 8 \times (-4) = -96$ _____

8. $-36 \times 4 - 4 = 0$ _____

9. $14 + (-1) + (-7) \div 3 = 2$ _____

10. $4 + 10 \div (-6) - 4 = 3$ _____

11. $16 \div 8 - 4 = 4$ _____

12. $6 + 3 \times (-2) = -18$ _____

NAME _____ DATE _____

5-10   NUMBERS IN BOXES

Choose integers from the list below. Place one in each box so that the answer is correct. You may only use an integer once in each problem (not including the given answer).

$$-1 \quad -2 \quad 3 \quad 4 \quad 5 \quad 6$$

1. $\dfrac{\square}{\square} + \dfrac{\square}{\square} = 1\dfrac{1}{4}$

2. $\dfrac{\square}{\square} - \dfrac{\square}{\square} = -\dfrac{1}{2}$

3. $\dfrac{\square}{\square} \times \dfrac{\square}{\square} = \dfrac{1}{6}$

4. $\dfrac{\square}{\square} \div \dfrac{\square}{\square} = -4\dfrac{1}{2}$

5. $\square\dfrac{\square}{\square} - \dfrac{\square}{\square} = -2\dfrac{1}{2}$

6. $\square\dfrac{\square}{\square} \times \dfrac{\square}{\square} = 9\dfrac{1}{5}$

5–11 PUTTING THE FUN IN FUNCTIONS

A value is placed in one of the functions below. Identify the function that has the given value.

$f(x) = 3x - 4$	$g(x) = x^2$
$h(x) = x^2 - 5$	$k(x) = (x-1)^2$

1. _____ $(7) = 36$

2. _____ $(-1) = 1$

3. _____ $(0) = -4$

4. _____ $(5) = 16$

5. _____ $(6) = 14$

6. _____ $(-2) = 9$

7. _____ $(4) = 8$

8. _____ $(-3) = -13$

9. _____ $(2) = 4$

10. _____ $(1) = -4$

11. _____ $(6) = 36$

12. _____ $(-5) = 36$

13. _____ $(2) +$ _____ $(2) = 1$

14. _____ $(-3) -$ _____ $(-3) = 12$

15. _____ $(-4) -$ _____ $(-4) = 41$

16. _____ $(-6) -$ _____ $(-6) = 5$

NAME _____ DATE _____

5-12 FINDING THE FOURTH

Each set of values for x and y below is determined by a set of rules. Three sets are given; the fourth is missing. Select the fourth set of values from the Answer Bank that follows the same rule as the previous three. Then state the rule. The first one is done for you.

	Sets of Values		Rule
1.	(3,4); (5,6); (15,16);	*(20,21)*	*y = x + 1*
2.	(0,0); (4,16); (10,100);	_____	_____
3.	(3,6); (10,20); (15,30);	_____	_____
4.	(0,–1); (5,4); (–1,–2);	_____	_____
5.	(15,12); (10,7); (–1,–4);	_____	_____
6.	(7,11); (–1,–5); (10,17);	_____	_____
7.	(–1,2); (4,17); (–3,10);	_____	_____
8.	(3,10); (–4,–11); (0,1);	_____	_____
9.	(4,–2); (10,–5); (–18,9);	_____	_____
10.	(2,16); (–3,36); (5,100);	_____	_____

Answer Bank

(–6,–15)	(–10,–13)	(–4,64)	(20,40)	(–5,26)
(5,16)	(7,49)	(–10,5)	(20,21)	(–5,–6)

NAME _____   DATE _____

5-13 ABSOLUTELY SURE!

Choose an answer from the Answer Bank to make the statement true. Each answer will be used only once.

Answer Bank
10
6
-30
-7
4
-19
12
8
-6
-9
0
1
5
15
-10

1. $|4| = $ _____

2. $|-6| = $ _____

3. $|10| = $ _____

4. $-|7| = $ _____

5. $|5 + 10| = $ _____

6. $|4 - 3| = $ _____

7. $|8| + |-4| = $ _____

8. $2|-6 + 2| = $ _____

9. $-|9| - |-10| = $ _____

10. $-|-6| = $ _____

11. $|-3 + 10| - |4 + 12| = $ _____

12. $-5|-6| = $ _____

13. $-3|-7| + |11| = $ _____

14. $|-6 + 7| - |1| = $ _____

15. $|8 - 12| + |7 - 6| = $ _____

NAME _____ DATE _____

5-14 THE LUCKY 13

Each blank in the equations below can be filled with a variable that completes the equation correctly. Replace each blank with the appropriate variable. Some problems have more than one solution.

$$a = 3 \qquad b = 0 \qquad c = -1 \qquad d = -6 \qquad e = 10 \qquad f = -2$$

1. $4\underline{\quad} = 0$

2. $\underline{\quad} \times \underline{\quad} = -6$

3. $\underline{\quad} + \underline{\quad} = 2$

4. $\underline{\quad} - \underline{\quad} = -16$

5. $\underline{\quad}(\underline{\quad} - \underline{\quad}) = 9$

6. $\underline{\quad} \times \underline{\quad} = -18$

7. $\underline{\quad} \times \underline{\quad} \times \underline{\quad} = 36$

8. $\dfrac{\underline{\quad} \times \underline{\quad}}{\underline{\quad}} = 2$

9. $\underline{\quad}\dfrac{}{\underline{\quad}} = -8$

10. $\underline{\quad}\dfrac{}{\underline{\quad}} = -1$

11. $\underline{\quad} = \underline{\quad} \div \underline{\quad}$

12. $\underline{\quad} \div \underline{\quad} = \underline{\quad} - \underline{\quad}$

13. $\underline{\quad} - \underline{\quad} = \underline{\quad} + \underline{\quad}$

NAME _____   DATE _____

5-15   AN EQUATION CHAIN

Solve the equations by substituting the solution for the variable in the next-numbered problem. You will have completed the chain correctly if the values for a in problems 1 and 14 are the same.

1. $3a = 15$

2. $6 + a = b$

3. $b - c = 7$

4. $\frac{d}{c} = 3$

5. $e + 5 = d$

6. $2e = f$

7. $f - g = 10$

8. $\frac{g}{2} = h$

9. $hi = 6$

10. $10 - j = i$

11. $\frac{k}{j} = 2$

12. $l + k = 26$

13. $l + m = 22$

14. $\frac{m}{2} = a$

NAME _____ DATE _____

5-16 MATCHING EQUATIONS

Solve each equation, write its solution, and find the pairs of equations that share the same solution.

1. $x - 1.4 = 9.2$ _____

2. $8 = x + 4.2$ _____

3. $x - (-0.7) = 4.5$ _____

4. $-6.8 + 4.25 = x$ _____

5. $-1.6x = 9.6$ _____

6. $-10.6 = -x$ _____

7. $\dfrac{x}{-7} = 2$ _____

8. $\dfrac{x}{8} = 3$ _____

9. $\dfrac{3}{5}x = -6$ _____

10. $\dfrac{x}{8} = -2\dfrac{1}{4}$ _____

11. $-40x = 560$ _____

12. $x + 11 = 1$ _____

13. $-7.6 = x - 5.05$ _____

14. $2.4 = -0.4x$ _____

15. $-12 = \dfrac{2}{3}x$ _____

16. $-2.4x = 1.2$ _____

17. $\dfrac{1}{4}x = 6$ _____

18. $5.9 + x = 5.4$ _____

5-17 NOT QUITE RIGHT

Some of the equations below have the correct solutions, but others have incorrect answers. Find the equations that are solved incorrectly and correct them.

Work Space

1. $28 - x + 4x = 7$
    $x = -7$

2. $2(x + 4) = 8$
    $x = 2$

3. $-4 - (2 + 3x) = 18$
    $x = 7$

4. $x + 7x = -32$
    $x = -4$

5. $-2(3 + x) + 5x = -24$
    $x = -6$

6. $2x + 5 = -x + 4$
    $x = 3$

7. $2x - 5 = 8x + 7$
    $x = -2$

8. $4x - 10 = x + 3x - 2x$
    $x = -2$

9. $-5(3x - 2) + 6(2 - 2x) = 3x$
    $x = 3.\overline{6}$

10. $14x - 1 = -3(1 - 2x) + 12$
    $x = 1\frac{1}{4}$

NAME _____ DATE _____

5–18 CORRECT SOLUTIONS

Each equation is missing at least one pair of grouping symbols. Rewrite the equation, inserting the parentheses so that the solution is correct.

1. $3x + 7 = 27$ $x = 2$ _____

2. $2x^2 = 36$ $x = 3$ _____

3. $3 - x + 4 = -8$ $x = 7$ _____

4. $1 = x + 1^0$ $x = $ all real numbers   _____

5. $15 \div x - 3 = 3$ $x = 8$ _____

6. $x + 4 \div x - 20 = -5$ $x = 16$ _____

7. $2 + x - 3x + 1 = 11$ $x = -5$ _____

8. $3x + 3 = 3x + 1$ $x = $ all real numbers   _____

9. $2x + 4x + 1 = 18$ $x = 1$ _____

10. $3x \div x - 1 = \phi$ $x = 1$ _____

NAME _____ DATE _____

5-19   GET TO THE POINT!

Identify the point or groups of points described below.

1. This point is called the origin. _____

2. The abscissa is zero and the ordinate is all real numbers for these points.

   _____

3. The ordinate is zero and the abscissa is all real numbers for these points.

   _____

4. The abscissa and ordinate are both positive for these points.

   _____

5. The abscissa and ordinate have opposite signs for these points.

   _____

6. The abscissa equals the ordinate for these points.

   _____

7. A line with a negative slope that contains the origin also contains these points.

   _____

8. The y-intercept is 5 and the x values are all real numbers for these points.

   _____

9. Each value of y is the opposite of the value of x for these points.

   _____

10. This point is on every line that has a y-intercept of zero. _____

NAME _____   DATE _____

5–20 COMMON KNOWLEDGE

All of the equations, terms, or points in each set below have something in common. Identify these common characteristics. Write your answers on the lines beneath the problems.

1. $y = 3x + 2$ $y = 7x + 9$ $y = -4x - 2$

_____

2. $2x = 3y$ $y = 4x$ $2x + 5y = 0$

_____

3. $y = 3x + 5$ $-4x + 2y = 4$ $-6y = -7x + 1$

_____

4. $4y = 0$ $3y = 1$ $-8y = 5$

_____

5. $4y = 4x - 2$ $x - y = \dfrac{1}{2}$ $y = x - \dfrac{1}{2}$

_____

6. m $\dfrac{rise}{run}$ $\dfrac{y_2 - y_1}{x_2 - x_1}$

_____

7. $y = 3x - 2$ $y = 7x - 2$ $y = -4x - 2$

_____

8. $(0,4)$ $(0,0)$ $(0,-2)$

_____

9. $(-3,-4)$ $(-8,-1)$ $(-1,-15)$

_____

10. $(0,2)$ $(-2,0)$ $(0,-2)$

_____

5–21   A SHINING STAR

Solve each system of equations, and graph the solutions on the grid at the bottom of the page. Connect the solutions in order from problems 1 through 5, and then connect the solution to problem 1.

1. $x + y = -6$
    $3x + 2y = -14$

2. $3x + 2y = 17$
    $x - y = 4$

3. $-x + y = 5$
    $x + 2y = -2$

4. $7x + 3y = 2$
    $2x + y = 0$

5. $4x - y = 0$
    $5x + y = 9$

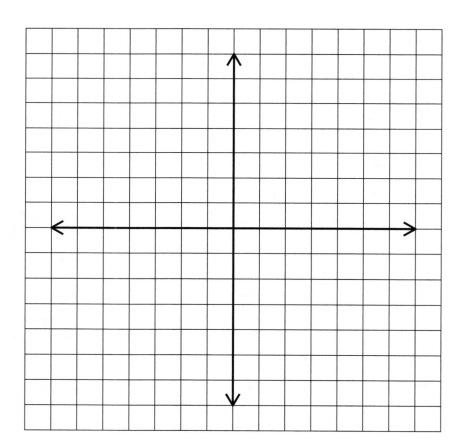

NAME _____ DATE _____

5-22 DOUBLETALK

Solve each system of equations. Then find the solution for each system in the Answer Bank. Each answer is used twice.

1. $x + y = 6$
   $x - y = 2$

2. $x + y = 10$
   $x - y = -4$

3. $x + y = 0$
   $x - y = -6$

4. $-7x + y = 1$
   $3 - 3y = 7x$

5. $x - y = 1$
   $y = 2x - 3$

6. $2x - y = -7$
   $x + 7 = y$

7. $x + y = 4$
   $3x - 2y = -13$

8. $-5x + 3y = -31$
   $-2x - 5y = 0$

9. $-3x + 4y = -6$
   $5x - 6y = 8$

10. $5x + 3y = 17$
    $2x - 9y = 17$

Answer Bank

| 1 | −3 | 2 | 0 | −1 | 3 | 7 | 5 | 4 | −2 |

NAME _____ DATE _____

5–23 A RADICAL CHANGE

Each of the radicals that follows is either not simplified or simplified incorrectly. Simplify and/or correct each radical.

1. $\sqrt{32} = \sqrt{16}\sqrt{2}$ _____

2. $\sqrt{18} = 2\sqrt{3}$ _____

3. $\sqrt{16} = \sqrt{4}$ _____

4. $\sqrt{24} = \sqrt{8}\sqrt{3}$ _____

5. $\sqrt{120} = \sqrt{8}\sqrt{15}$ _____

6. $\sqrt{12} = 3\sqrt{2}$ _____

7. $\sqrt{144} = \sqrt{12}\sqrt{12}$ _____

8. $\sqrt{28} = \sqrt{2}\sqrt{14}$ _____

9. $\sqrt{98} = 2\sqrt{7}$ _____

10. $\sqrt{150} = 6\sqrt{5}$ _____

NAME _____   DATE _____

5-24   RADICAL MATCHES

Each problem in the column on the left has the same answer as a problem in the column on the right. Solve the problems, and circle the numbers of the problems that have the same answer.

1. $\sqrt{98} - \sqrt{8} =$

11. $\sqrt{6} \cdot \sqrt{8} =$

2. $\sqrt{24} - \sqrt{6} =$

12. $4\sqrt{3} + \sqrt{48} =$

3. $\sqrt{27} + \sqrt{3} =$

13. $\sqrt{5} \cdot \sqrt{10} =$

4. $15 \div \sqrt{3} =$

14. $4\sqrt{15} \div \sqrt{3} =$

5. $\sqrt{2}\left(\sqrt{3} + \sqrt{6}\right) =$

15. $\sqrt{6} + \sqrt{12} =$

6. $3\sqrt{5} + \sqrt{5} =$

16. $\sqrt{20} + \sqrt{45} =$

7. $\sqrt{8} + \sqrt{12} =$

17. $\sqrt{18} \div \sqrt{3} =$

8. $\sqrt{50} - \sqrt{32} =$

18. $2 \div \sqrt{2} =$

9. $8\sqrt{6} \div \sqrt{2} =$

19. $\sqrt{75} =$

10. $10\sqrt{5} \div 2 =$

20. $2\left(\sqrt{2} + \sqrt{3}\right) =$

NAME _____ DATE _____

5-25 ALL IN THE RANGE

Solve each equation. All of the solutions are less than or equal to −10 and no larger than 10.

1. $x^2 = 100$

2. $(x-1)^2 = 49$

3. $(x+3)^2 = 9$

4. $x^2 - 16 = 0$

5. $5x^2 = 125$

6. $(3x+2)^2 = 4$

7. $\left(x + \frac{2}{3}\right)^2 = \frac{1}{64}$

8. $3(x-5)^2 = 75$

9. $5(2x-1)^2 = 45$

10. $\frac{x^2}{2} - 1 = \frac{1}{8}$

NAME _____ DATE _____

5-26 AND THE ANSWER IS . . .

Each equation below has at least one real solution; some have two. Match each equation with its solution(s) from the Answer Bank. Each answer is used only once.

1. $x^2 - 2x + 1 = 0$

_____

2. $x^2 + 2x - 15 = 0$

_____

3. $x^2 - 8x + 16 = 0$

_____

4. $-2x^2 - 3x + 2 = 0$

_____

5. $-x^2 + 3 = 0$

_____

6. $x^2 - x = 3$

_____

7. $x^2 + 3x = 3$

_____

8. $x^2 + 4x = -3$

_____

9. $4x^2 = 25$

_____

10. $6x^2 + x = 12$

_____

Answer Bank

$$-\sqrt{3} \qquad \frac{-5}{2} \qquad -2 \qquad \frac{-3+\sqrt{21}}{2} \qquad 1 \qquad -1 \qquad 4 \qquad \frac{1-\sqrt{13}}{2} \qquad -3 \qquad \frac{4}{3}$$

$$\frac{1}{2} \qquad 3 \qquad \frac{5}{2} \qquad \frac{-3-\sqrt{21}}{2} \qquad \frac{-3}{2} \qquad -5 \qquad \sqrt{3} \qquad \frac{1+\sqrt{13}}{2}$$

5-27 VARYING VALUES

The value of the *discriminate*, $b^2 - 4ac$, indicates the number of real solutions of an equation. Each equation that follows is written in the correct form, but the values of *a*, *b*, and *c* are switched. Rearrange the values so that the equation has the designated number of solutions.

1. $7x^2 + x + 5 = 0$ **two real solutions**

2. $9x^2 + x - 6 = 0$ **one real solution**

3. $4x^2 + 5x - 1 = 0$ **no real solutions**

4. $25x^2 + 4x = 20$ **one real solution**

5. $4x^2 + 1 = -3x$ **two real solutions**

6. $4x^2 + x = 0$ **no real solutions**

NAME _____ DATE _____

5-28 COMMON TO BOTH

Each polynomial in the pairs below has a factor that is common to both. Identify this common factor.

1. $3x^2 + 6x + 15$ $3x^2 + 9x + 12$ _____

2. $x^3 + 2x^2 + x$ $2x^3 + 2x^2 + 2x$ _____

3. $2x^2y + 4xy + 2x$ $10x^2y + 8xy + 4x$ _____

4. $x^2 + 3x - 4$ $x^2 - 16$ _____

5. $x^2 + 10x + 9$ $x^2 + 7x - 18$ _____

6. $x^2 + 5x + 6$ $x^2 + x - 6$ _____

7. $x^2 - 6x + 8$ $x^2 - 7x + 10$ _____

8. $3x^2 - 11x - 4$ $3x^2 + 16x + 5$ _____

9. $12x^2 - 13x + 3$ $8x^2 + 14x - 15$ _____

10. $6x^2 - 18x + 12$ $4x^2 - 6x - 4$ _____

NAME _____ DATE _____

5-29 SOMETHING'S WRONG

Some of the inequalities below are solved incorrectly. Identify those solutions that are incorrect, and correct them. **Hint:** There are more incorrect solutions than correct ones.

1. $x - 3 > 4$
    $x > 7$

2. $x + 4 < 6$
    $x < -2$

3. $2x - 1 \geq 5$
    $x > 3$

4. $-4x - 5 < 11$
    $x < -4$

5. $x - 4 \geq -10$
    $x \geq -6$

6. $3x + 4 > 19$
    $x > 15$

7. $x - 7 \geq 3$
    $x > 10$

8. $12 - x > 2$
    $x < 10$

9. $4x - 3 > x + 6$
    $x < 3$

10. $-2x - 4 \leq -x - 1$
    $x \geq -3$

11. $2x - 5 \geq -9$
    $x \leq -2$

12. $8x + 7 < -9$
    $x < -2$

NAME _____   DATE _____

5–30 ABSOLUTELY CORRECT

Solve each equation or inequality. You will find your answers in the Answer Bank. Each answer will be used only once.

1. $|x| = 7$

2. $|x| = -3$

3. $|x| < 6$

4. $|x| \geq 8$

5. $2|x| = 10$

6. $|x + 4| = 10$

7. $|x - 5| \leq 10$

8. $|x + 9| < 8$

9. $|x + 3| > 6$

10. $|3x + 1| = 13$

11. $|2x - 1| < 10$

12. $|3x + 4| > 11$

Answer Bank

$$x = -4\frac{2}{3} \qquad x > 3 \qquad x > 2\frac{1}{3} \qquad x \geq -5 \qquad x > -6 \qquad x = -5 \qquad x = 7 \qquad x < 6$$

$$x = -14 \qquad x = -7 \qquad x > -17 \qquad \phi \qquad x \geq 8 \qquad x < -1 \qquad x \leq -8 \qquad x = 4$$

$$x > -4\frac{1}{2} \qquad x = 5 \qquad x \leq 15 \qquad x < -9 \qquad x = 6 \qquad x < -5 \qquad x < 5\frac{1}{2}$$

NAME _____ DATE _____

5–31   FIND THE FUNCTIONS

Find $f(x)$ and $g(x)$ so that $(f \circ g)(x)$ and $(g \circ f)(x)$ are correct.

1. $(f \circ g)(x) = (x + 2)^2$ $\qquad\qquad\qquad (g \circ f)(x) = x^2 + 2$

2. $(f \circ g)(x) = \sqrt{x} - 7$ $\qquad\qquad\qquad (g \circ f)(x) = \sqrt{x - 7}$

3. $(f \circ g)(x) = x - 7$ $\qquad\qquad\qquad (g \circ f)(x) = x - 7$

4. $(f \circ g)(x) = x^2 - 2$ $\qquad\qquad\qquad (g \circ f)(x) = x^2 - 2x$

5. $(f \circ g)(x) = x^2 - 2x + 1$ $\qquad\qquad\qquad (g \circ f)(x) = x^2 - 1$

6. $(f \circ g)(x) = 2x - 1$ $\qquad\qquad\qquad (g \circ f)(x) = 2x - 2$

NAME _____   DATE _____

5–32 RELATIVITY

Identify each family of functions from the following clues. Some problems have more than one answer.

$$y = x \qquad y = x^2 \qquad y = x^3 \qquad y = |x| \qquad y = \left[|x|\right] \qquad y = \frac{1}{x} \qquad y = \sqrt{x}$$

1. I am also called a quadratic function.

    _____

2. My range is all real numbers greater than or equal to 0.

    _____

3. I am a special type of step function.

    _____

4. I am symmetric to the y-axis.

    _____

5. I am symmetric to the line $y = x$.

    _____

6. I am symmetric to the origin.

    _____

7. My graph is in quadrants 1 and 3, and on the origin.

    _____

8. My graph does not include the origin.

    _____

9. There are no straight lines on my graph.

    _____

10. My range and domain are only positive numbers and 0.

    _____

NAME _____ DATE _____

5-33   JUST PASSING THROUGH

Visualize each graph, and write the quadrant(s) that it passes through.

1. $y = x$

   _____

2. $y = -|x|$

   _____

3. $y = x^2 + 1$

   _____

4. $y = -x^3$

   _____

5. $y = \left[|x + 4| \right]$

   _____

6. $y = \sqrt{x - 3}$

   _____

7. $y = \dfrac{1}{x}$

   _____

8. $y = -3x + 2$

   _____

9. $y = |x + 5|$

   _____

10. $y = (x - 3)^3 - 1$

    _____

11. $y = \sqrt{x + 7} + 1$

    _____

12. $y = (x + 4)^3$

    _____

13. $y = -\dfrac{1}{x + 3}$

    _____

14. $y = \left[|x| \right]$

    _____

15. $y = 3x^2 - 10$

    _____

16. $y = -\sqrt{x}$

    _____

5-34 DEFINING EXPRESSIONS

Some of the following mathematical expressions can be evaluated by substituting any real number; the expression will then be defined. Circle these expressions. If an expression cannot be evaluated by substituting any real number, find the *real* numbers that can be substituted and write them on the line.

1. $x^2 + 3x + 4$ _____

2. $\dfrac{1}{x}$ _____

3. $x + 7$ _____

4. $\dfrac{1}{x+8}$ _____

5. $x^2 + 1$ _____

6. $x^3 - 1$ _____

7. $\dfrac{1}{\sqrt{x}}$ _____

8. $\sqrt{x+3}$ _____

9. $\dfrac{1}{2x}$ _____

10. $4x - 8$ _____

11. $\dfrac{1}{x^2 - 4}$ _____

12. $x^2 - 4$ _____

13. $\sqrt{x-8}$ _____

14. $\dfrac{1}{x-8}$ _____

15. $\dfrac{3}{x^2 - 7x + 10}$ _____

NAME _____ DATE _____

5-35 HOW WELL DO YOU FUNCTION?

Fill in the blanks with the function(s) that will make each statement true. Include any restrictions on the variable(s) if necessary.

$$f(x) = x - 3 \qquad\qquad h(x) = x^2 - 1$$
$$g(x) = x^2 - 4x + 3 \qquad k(x) = x^2 - 2x - 3$$

1. $(f + \underline{\hspace{1cm}})(x) = x^2 + x - 4$

2. $(h - \underline{\hspace{1cm}})(x) = 4x - 4$

3. $(f \cdot \underline{\hspace{1cm}})(x) = x^3 - 3x^2 - x + 3$

4. $(\underline{\hspace{1cm}} \div f)(x) = \dfrac{x^2 - 1}{x - 3}$

5. $(g + \underline{\hspace{1cm}})(x) = x^2 - 3x$

6. $(g - \underline{\hspace{1cm}})(x) = -4x + 4$

7. $(h \cdot \underline{\hspace{1cm}})(x) = x^4 - 2x^3 - 4x^2 + 2x + 3$

8. $(k \div \underline{\hspace{1cm}})(x) = \dfrac{x + 1}{x - 1}$

9. $(\underline{\hspace{1cm}} + \underline{\hspace{1cm}})(x) = x^2 - x - 6$

10. $(\underline{\hspace{1cm}} - \underline{\hspace{1cm}})(x) = -2x + 6$

11. $(\underline{\hspace{1cm}} \cdot \underline{\hspace{1cm}})(x) = x^4 - 6x^3 + 8x^2 + 6x - 9$

12. $(\underline{\hspace{1cm}} \div \underline{\hspace{1cm}})(x) = \dfrac{x - 3}{x - 1}$

Section 6

DATA ANALYSIS

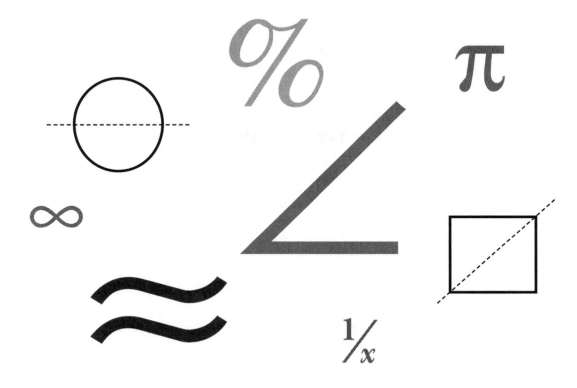

NAME _____ DATE _____

6–1 PASSING THE TEST

Each set of test scores was selected randomly from students in Mr. Rocha's science classes. The numbers in the Answer Bank represent the mean, median, and mode (in that order). Match the data in the Answer Bank with the scores with which they can be paired by writing the letter of your answer on the line in front of each set of scores.

1. _____ 95, 93, 80, 93, 94

2. _____ 85, 85, 84, 95, 85

3. _____ 100, 86, 80, 90, 84

4. _____ 90, 83, 97, 96

5. _____ 95, 87, 94, 95

6. _____ 94, 70, 70, 100

Answer Bank

A. 88, 86, none

B. 92.75, 90.5, 95

C. 86.8, 85, 85

D. 91, 93, 93

E. 83.5, 82, 70

F. 91.5, 93, none

NAME _____ DATE _____

6-2 INSERTING THE MISSING DATA

Place a number in each set so that the statement is true.

1. The mean is 85.   {95, 84, 90, 74, _____}

2. The mean is 87.   {86, 91, 94, 83, 75, _____}

3. 70 is the only mode.   {85, 96, 96, 70, 70, _____}

4. The median is 82.   {80, 80, 85, 90, _____}

5. The median is 91.   {82, 95, 89, _____}

6. The median remains the same.   {86, 81, 85, _____}

7. The mean remains the same.   {85, 84, 81, 86, _____}

8. There is only one mode and the mean is 89.   {92, 92, 87, 87, _____}

Work Space

NAME _____   DATE _____

6-3 CHARTING THE TEMPERATURES

The temperature in Happyburg is exciting and unpredictable. Chart the average temperature for last week on graph paper by following the clues. (All temperatures are in degrees Fahrenheit.)

1. The average temperature on Wednesday was 75°.

2. The average temperature on Wednesday had increased 6° from Tuesday.

3. The average temperature on Saturday and Sunday was the same. This average temperature was 1° more than the average temperature on Friday.

4. The average temperature on Friday was 4° more than it was on Wednesday.

5. The average temperature on Monday was 8° lower than it was on Friday.

6. Thursday's average temperature was 2° more than the average temperature on Friday.

NAME _____   DATE _____

6-4   A PIECE OF THE PIE

Find the amount of money Kathleen spent on each item by using the information below. Write your answers in the spaces provided.

Kathleen recently started a part-time job and decided to keep track of her expenses. She earns $400 a month by working after school and on weekends. She found that the monthly amount she paid for taxes, gas for her car, and miscellaneous expenses was the same. The amount of money she paid for clothing and entertainment (including movies) was the same, and each was twice the amount she spent on gas. Her cost for food and the cost of her phone bill were the same, each being $\frac{3}{4}$ of the amount spent on clothes.

Label each part of the graph, and then write the amount of money Kathleen pays each month for the following:

clothing = _____   gas = _____

entertainment = _____   food = _____

taxes = _____   phone = _____

miscellaneous expenses = _____

Kathleen's Monthly Budget

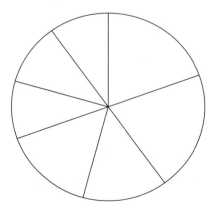

NAME _____ DATE _____

6-5 MARK THAT DATE

The dates of the days in the month of February are placed in a hat, drawn at random, and then replaced. Find the indicated probability in the Answer Bank and write the letter of the answer in the blank before the problem number. Read down the column to complete the statement at the end of the activity.

1. _____ P(number is even)

2. _____ P(number has only one digit)

3. _____ P(number ends in 6)

4. _____ P(number is a multiple of 10)

5. _____ P(number is a multiple of 5)

6. _____ P(number is prime)

7. _____ P(number is a multiple of 3)

8. _____ P(number ends in 5)

9. _____ P(number is a multiple of 13)

10. _____ P(number is a multiple of 7)

11. _____ P(number is neither prime nor composite)

12. _____ P(number has a hyphen when it is spelled)

13. _____ P(number ends in a 0 or 5)

14. _____ P(number has two digits)

15. _____ P(number ends in 4)

February

1	2	3	4	5	6	7
8	9	10	11	12	13	14
15	16	17	18	19	20	21
22	23	24	25	26	27	28

Answer Bank

T. $\frac{1}{7}$

E. $\frac{3}{28}$

R. $\frac{9}{28}$

O. $\frac{5}{28}$

A. $\frac{1}{2}$

I. $\frac{1}{28}$

C. $\frac{1}{14}$

S. $\frac{2}{7}$

N. $\frac{19}{28}$

The probability that all of your answers ___ ___ ___   ___ ___ ___ ___ ___ ___ ___

___ ___   ___ ___ ___.

NAME _____ DATE _____

6–6 ALL ABOUT DATA

We are constantly bombarded by data. A few ways to organize and represent data are listed below. Unfortunately, the words have been scrambled. Use the clues to help you unscramble the following words related to data.

1. **arb pargh:** data composed by lengths of bars _____

2. **pha ipegr:** also called a circle graph _____

3. **thicgrpoap:** symbols used to represent data _____

4. **amtergrscat:** information represented by unconnected points

   _____

5. **ureqefc nablety:** table used to organize data

   _____

6. **enln tirde:** also called the line of best fit _____

7. **som-dpet-lanlefta:** also can be part of a plant

   _____

8. **hamiogtsr:** type of bar graph that displays frequency of data _____

9. **ring leaph:** displays data as points connected by line segments _____

10. **erao-wplhnb-isxd kot:** displays median of a set of data and median of each half of the

    data _____

6-7   A MATRIX CHAIN

Add or subtract the matrices, using the answer to each problem as the next link in the chain. Then answer the question at the bottom of the page.

1.
$$\overset{A}{\begin{bmatrix} 2 & -3 & 4 \\ 6 & 1 & 2 \end{bmatrix}} + \overset{B}{\begin{bmatrix} 3 & 0 & 5 \\ 2 & 7 & -4 \end{bmatrix}} = \overset{C}{\begin{bmatrix} & & \end{bmatrix}}$$

2.
$$\overset{C}{\begin{bmatrix} & & \end{bmatrix}} - \overset{D}{\begin{bmatrix} 1 & 4 & 2 \\ 10 & 4 & -1 \end{bmatrix}} = \overset{E}{\begin{bmatrix} & & \end{bmatrix}}$$

3.
$$\overset{E}{\begin{bmatrix} & & \end{bmatrix}} - \overset{F}{\begin{bmatrix} 2 & -4 & 8 \\ -7 & -1 & -3 \end{bmatrix}} = \overset{G}{\begin{bmatrix} & & \end{bmatrix}}$$

4.
$$\overset{H}{\begin{bmatrix} -3 & 2 & 4 \\ -6 & 0 & -3 \end{bmatrix}} + \overset{G}{\begin{bmatrix} & & \end{bmatrix}} = \overset{I}{\begin{bmatrix} & & \end{bmatrix}}$$

5.
$$\overset{I}{\begin{bmatrix} & & \end{bmatrix}} - \overset{M}{\begin{bmatrix} -3 & 2 & -1 \\ -7 & 4 & -3 \end{bmatrix}} = \overset{K}{\begin{bmatrix} & & \end{bmatrix}}$$

Which matrices are equal? _____

NAME _____   DATE _____

6-8   THE MISSING ELEMENTS

Numbers are missing from some matrices below. Find the missing numbers.

Work Space

1. $3\begin{bmatrix} 4 & 3 \\ -2 & 6 \end{bmatrix} = \begin{bmatrix} 12 & \underline{\quad} \\ \underline{\quad} & 18 \end{bmatrix}$

2. $\begin{bmatrix} 3 & -7 \end{bmatrix}\begin{bmatrix} 2 \\ -3 \end{bmatrix} = \begin{bmatrix} \underline{\quad} \end{bmatrix}$

3. $\begin{bmatrix} -3 & -1 \\ 5 & -2 \end{bmatrix}\begin{bmatrix} 5 \\ -2 \end{bmatrix} = \begin{bmatrix} -13 \\ \underline{\quad} \end{bmatrix}$

4. $\begin{bmatrix} 2 & 3 \\ -4 & 1 \end{bmatrix}\begin{bmatrix} -3 & 2 \\ -5 & -1 \end{bmatrix} = \begin{bmatrix} \underline{\quad} & 1 \\ 7 & \underline{\quad} \end{bmatrix}$

5. $\begin{bmatrix} -4 & 5 \\ 7 & -2 \\ -5 & 3 \end{bmatrix}\begin{bmatrix} -2 & 4 \\ 3 & 1 \end{bmatrix} = \begin{bmatrix} 23 & \underline{\quad} \\ \underline{\quad} & 26 \\ \underline{\quad} & -17 \end{bmatrix}$

NAME _____ DATE _____

6–9 THE ODDS ARE . . .

Find the probability and odds of each event.

1. Randomly selecting a king from a deck of fifty-two cards.
    Probability: **Odds:**

2. Randomly selecting a number ending in zero from the first one hundred numbers.
    Probability: **Odds:**

3. Randomly selecting a B from the letters in PROBABILITY.
    Probability: **Odds:**

4. Randomly selecting a square number from the first ten numbers.
    Probability: **Odds:**

5. Randomly selecting a four from the first five digits.
    Probability: **Odds:**

6. Randomly selecting a pencil from a container holding six pencils and four pens.
    Probability: **Odds:**

7. Randomly selecting a month that has thirty days from a calendar containing each month of the year.
    Probability: **Odds:**

8. Randomly selecting a black sock from a drawer containing four black socks and nine blue socks.
    Probability: **Odds:**

9. Randomly selecting a prime number from a list of the digits from zero to nine inclusive.
    Probability: **Odds:**

10. Randomly selecting a day that starts with T from the days of the week.
    Probability: **Odds:**

Section 7

POTPOURRI

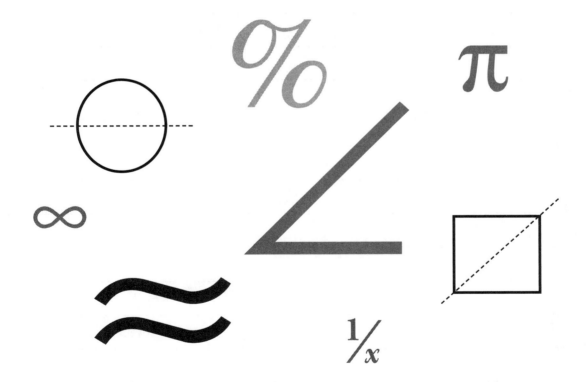

NAME _____ DATE _____

7-1   DEUCES ARE WILD

Many numbers can be written in a variety of ways. Using the numbers 1, 3, 4, 5, 6, 7, 8, and 9, write as many ways as you can to arrive at 2. A given number may be used only once within each equation. Two examples are done for you.

$$10 \div 5 = 2 \qquad (5 \times 4) \div (9 + 1) = 2$$

_____

_____

_____

_____

_____

_____

_____

_____

_____

_____

_____

_____

_____

_____

NAME _____   DATE _____

7-2 FINDING MISSING NUMBERS

Use the clues to find the missing numbers.

1. Half of this two-digit number is 3 times half of 28. This number is _____.

2. A third of this three-digit number is 5 times 20 plus 7. This number is _____.

3. This two-digit number is one-fourth of one-tenth of a thousand. This number is

   _____.

4. This two-digit number is 2 times 40 percent of 120. This number is _____.

5. This three-digit number plus 58 is half of 618 less 8. This number is _____.

6. This one-digit number is one-fifth of 30 minus 2 squared. This number is _____.

7. A fourth of this five-digit number is 5 times one-third of 99 plus half of 5,240. This

   number is _____.

8. This two-digit number is 4 times 46 divided by the difference of 16 minus 75 percent

   of 16. This number is _____.

9. This three-digit number is 5 times 4 cubed. This number is _____.

10. This four-digit number is a fourth of 4,000 plus the difference between 20 and 10. This

    number is _____.

NAME _____   DATE _____

7-3   MAKE A QUIZ

Pretend you are the teacher of a math class and it is time for a quiz. Make a quiz of eight problems on topics you are currently studying or have studied. Vary your problems; be sure to keep an answer key. Maybe your teacher will let you give your quiz to some of your classmates.

1.   5.

2.   6.

3.   7.

4.   8.

7-4   READING THE SIGNS

Place a +, −, ×, or ÷ sign between the numbers to equal the given answer. Write the new equation on the line. The first one is done for you.

1. 4 8 9 2 3 7 5 = 5,267

$$4,892 + 375 = 5,267$$

2. 4 0 7 4 4 2 = 97

3. 5 2 7 4 2 8 = 147,672

4. 9 0 0 5 2 4 7 5 8 = 85,294

5. 3 9 1 5 3 9 3 = 421

6. 2 7 9 5 8 6 3 9 = 11,434

7. 2 7 6 4 5 7 = 126,132

8. 5 3 2 7 8 6 9 5 3 = 46,325

9. 9 6 7 8 1 5 2 = 1,471,056

10. 9 9 5 2 5 0 3 7 5 = 2,654

NAME _____ DATE _____

7-5 WHEELING AROUND

Complete each number wheel according to the given operation. Starting with the number at the center of each wheel, perform the indicated operation to complete the open parts of the wheel. An example in the first wheel is given. Starting at the center and working outward, 221 + 45 = 266. Complete each wheel in the same manner. Some answers will require working backwards.

1.

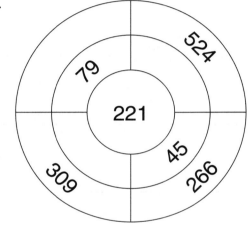

Addition

2.

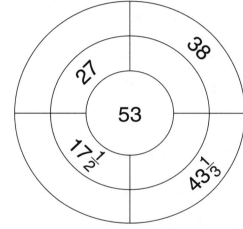

Subtraction

3.

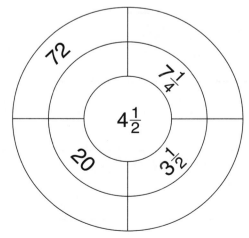

Multiplication

4.

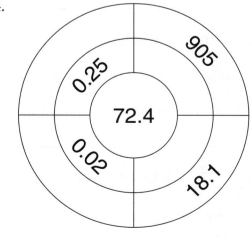

Division

NAME _____ DATE _____

7–6   MATH TIC-TAC-TOE

To win the game, follow the directions.

1. Place an X on the values that equal $\frac{3}{5}$.

$\frac{6}{10}$	60%	0.06
6 dimes	$\frac{4}{5} - \frac{1}{5}$	$\frac{2}{5} \times \frac{3}{2}$
4 out of 10	$\frac{2}{5} \div \frac{3}{2}$	$\frac{6}{100}$

2. Place an X on the values that equal $\frac{1}{3}$ of a quantity.

4 eggs	15 min	$33\frac{1}{3}\%$
3 dimes	30 cm	20 min
6 out of 18	$0.4 - 0.1$	$\frac{1}{2} \times \frac{2}{3}$

3. Create a tic-tac-toe board of your own so that you can win by placing an X on values that equal $\frac{1}{4}$.

NAME _____   DATE _____

7–7   IT'S A DATE

Some important dates in the history of mathematics are written in Roman numerals. Rewrite them on the lines in the number system we use today.

1. **DXXX** B.C.   Pythagoras and the Pythagoreans try to find a mathematical reason for all events in the universe.   _____

2. **CCC** B.C.   Euclid completes *Elements,* a thirteen-volume work devoted to geometry, algebra, and number theory.   _____

3. **C** A.D.   Astronomers begin to develop trigonometry.   _____

4. **CC**   Diophantus develops algebra.   _____

5. **DC**   The idea of zero is introduced.   _____

6. **MCDLXXVII**   The first mathematics books are printed.   _____

7. **MCDLXXXIX**   + and − are introduced.   _____

8. **MD**   Negative numbers are introduced.   _____

9. **MDXL**   Imaginary numbers are explored.   _____

10. **MDLXXX**   Decimals are introduced.   _____

11. **MDCXXX**   The coordinate plane is introduced.   _____

12. **MDCL**   Pascal invents the first adding machine.   _____

13. **MDCLXXX**   Leibniz works on calculus.   _____

14. **MDCCCX**   Gauss explores number theory.   _____

15. **MDCCCXL**   Mathematicians work with matrices, vectors, and logic.   _____

16. **MCMV**   Albert Einstein develops the Theory of Relativity.   _____

17. **MCMXVI**   Waclaw Sierpiński introduces what later became known as the Sierpiński Triangle.   _____

18. **MCMXLV**   Mathematicians/researchers work with computers.   _____

19. **MCMLXXVI**   Benoit Mandlebrot coins the term *fractal.*   _____

20. **MCMXCV**   Andrew Wiles proves Fermat's last theorem.   _____

NAME _____ DATE _____

7–8 LEFT TO RIGHT OR RIGHT TO LEFT

Follow the directions and answer the questions. (More than one answer may be possible.)

1. Add a number to 32.41 so that the sum is a palindrome. What is the number to be added, and what is the palindrome? _____

2. Subtract a number from 937 so that the difference is a palindrome. What is the number to be subtracted, and what is the palindrome? _____

3. Multiply 11 by a two-digit number so that the product is a palindrome. What is the two-digit number, and what is the palindrome? _____

4. Divide 440 by a one-digit number so that the quotient is a palindrome. What is the one-digit number, and what is the palindrome? _____

5. Add two proper fractions so that the numerator and denominator of the sum are both palindromes. What are the fractions, and what is the sum? _____

6. Divide a three-digit palindrome by 2 so that the quotient is a palindrome. What is the original number and the quotient? _____

7. The area of a square is a palindrome. What is the length of the side?

_____

8. The perimeter of a triangle is a palindrome. What are the lengths of the sides?

_____

NAME _____ DATE _____

7–9 WHAT'S THE PROBLEM?

For each question below, write a word problem on another sheet of paper. Then solve the problem.

1. What was Romero's average on his three math tests?

2. What was the total cost of the four items, including a 6% sales tax?

3. What was the total cost of the carpeting?

4. How much of a tip should Marisa leave?

5. What score does Charles have to get on his fourth science test if he wants to have a 90 test average?

6. What was the cost of the CD player after the price was reduced 20%?

7. What was the percent of increase in Joe's pay?

8. What was the unit price of the paper plates?

9. Which was the better buy? The stereo at Sounds Good or the same stereo at CostLess?

10. How much change did Danny receive from a $20 bill?

7-10   AND THE QUESTION IS . . .

Answers are provided below. Write a word problem for each answer.

1. $2.50

2. 25%

3. $\frac{1}{8}$

4. 60 mph

5. $\frac{1}{6}$

6. 120 square feet

7. $1\frac{1}{2}$ hours

8. 45°

9. 360 miles

10. $1.29 per pound

NAME_____ DATE_____

7-11 YOU'RE THE TEACHER

A student answered each problem incorrectly. Explain how the student arrived at the incorrect answers. Use the back of this sheet for your answers.

1. Joe purchased a CD for $11.99 and two CD cases for $0.99 each. How much change did he receive from $20? **Answer:** $13.97

2. The soccer team won four out of five games they played. Find the ratio of wins to losses. **Answer:** 4 to 5

3. Find the total bill if Alyssa bought a purse for $18.99 and a belt for $8.99. The sales tax was 6%. **Answer:** $29.65

4. Carpeting sells for $25.99 a square yard. Find the cost of carpeting a nine-foot-by-twelve-foot room. **Answer:** $2,806.92

5. Find the area of a circle with a radius of 9 inches. **Answer:** 56.52 square inches

6. A dress originally sold for $100. At first it was on sale at 10% off. A few weeks later it was reduced another 10%. Find the cost of the dress. **Answer:** $80

7. Find the number of square inches in a square foot. **Answer:** 12

8. John and his two friends went out for lunch. The bill, including a tip and sales tax, came to $14.46. They decided to split the cost evenly. How much did each person pay? **Answer:** $7.23

9. Cassandra traveled to her aunt's house at a rate of 60 miles per hour and traveled for three hours. Before she returned home, she stopped at a friend's house. She traveled at a rate of 40 miles per hour for one hour. Find her average speed for the day's travel. **Answer:** 50 miles per hour

10. Cory bought six spiral notebooks on sale for two for $1.50, a package of loose-leaf paper for $0.99, and one pack of compact discs for $5.99. Find the total cost. **Answer:** $15.98

NAME _____ DATE _____

7-12 FINDING MISSING INFORMATION

In each word problem below, information is missing. Supply the missing information so that the problem is valid.

1. Josh works part-time after school and on Saturday afternoons in a local convenience store. Last week he worked _____ hours and earned $89.60. How much is Josh paid per hour? **Answer:** $6.40

2. Last night Janine worked _____ minutes on her math homework. She worked 25 minutes on history and _____ minutes on science. How long did Janine work on homework last night? **Answer:** 1 hour and 10 minutes

3. Eduardo is saving money to buy a new bike, which costs $525.95. He has already saved $362. Last week he earned $_____ mowing lawns and $_____ for helping Mr. Thomas clean out his garage. How much does Eduardo still need to buy the bike? **Answer:** $53.95

4. For Cassie's birthday, her mother bought concert tickets for Cassie and two of her friends. Each ticket cost $_____, plus an additional $_____ service charge. How much did Cassie's mother pay for the tickets in all? **Answer:** $217.50

5. Peter went shopping. He bought a pair of jeans for $_____, a sweater for $_____, and a shirt for $18.99. How much did he pay for these clothes? **Answer:** $68.97

NAME _____ DATE _____

7-13   CREATE A PATTERN

Starting with the first number in each set, create a pattern that leads to the last number. The first one is done for you.

1. 9, _____ 7 _____, _____ 5 _____, _____ 3 _____, 1

2. $2\frac{1}{2}$, _____, _____, _____, $4\frac{1}{2}$

3. 100, _____, _____, _____, 20

4. 3.25, _____, _____, _____, 1.25

5. 5, _____, _____, _____, 3,125

6. 4, _____, _____, _____, 5

7. 80, _____, _____, _____, 90

8. 4, _____, _____, _____, 36

9. 42, _____, _____, _____, 22

10. 1, _____, _____, _____, 0.0001

11. $\frac{1}{2}$, _____, _____, _____, $\frac{1}{6}$

12. $\frac{1}{2}$, _____, _____, _____, $\frac{5}{6}$

NAME _____ DATE _____

7-14 SIGNS

Provide the signs to make the equations valid. You may need to use parentheses for some problems.

1. 8 ___ 4 ___ 3 = 29

2. 24 ___ 8 ___ 5 = 15

3. 9 ___ 4 ___ 6 = 6

4. 8 ___ 4 ___ 3 = 4

5. 9 ___ 7 ___ 2 ___ 3 = 10

6. 25 ___ 5 ___ 3 ___ 1 = 5

7. 7 ___ 2 ___ 4 ___ 2 = 16

8. 4 ___ 4 ___ 2 ___ 8 = 0

9. 6 ___ 3 ___ 8 ___ 4 = 6

10. 12 ___ 6 ___ 7 ___ 5 = 12

NAME DATE

7–15 NUMBERS AND VALUES

Match each term with an equivalent form. Choose your answers from the Answer Bank.

1. $\dfrac{1}{4}$ = _____

2. 80% = _____

3. 19 = _____

4. 3^2 = _____

5. $\sqrt{64}$ = _____

6. 7.5 = _____

7. 0.3 = _____

8. $\dfrac{27}{4}$ = _____

9. 1 = _____

10. $16\dfrac{1}{3}\%$ = _____

11. 13 = _____

12. $\dfrac{1}{20}$ = _____

Answer Bank

$4^2 + 3$

$\dfrac{1}{6}$

0.05

$2^2 + 2^2$

25%

$4 \text{ out of } 5$

$\dfrac{3}{10}$

$2^2 + 3^2$

$2^3 + 1$

$\dfrac{15}{2}$

100%

$6\dfrac{3}{4}$

NAME _____ DATE _____

7–16   A MIXED-UP MAGIC SQUARE

A magic square is a group of numbers arranged such that the sum of the numbers in each row, column, and diagonal is the same. This sum is called the magic number.

   The square below is not so magical. Only one row and one column add up to the magic number. Rearrange the other numbers to make a magic square.

10	16	14	13
12	6	7	9
1	8	11	5
4	3	2	15

What's the magic number? _____

NAME _____ DATE _____

7-17   MATH WORD CHAINS

List as many related mathematical words as you can for each of the topics below. Of course, there is a catch. The ending letter of each word in each list must be the beginning letter of the next word. When you are done, compare the math chains. Be sure to note that some words appear in different lists—evidence of how various topics in math are related.

Whole Numbers

_____

_____

_____

_____

_____

_____

_____

_____

_____

_____

_____

_____

_____

_____

_____

_____

_____

_____

_____

Fractions

_____

_____

_____

_____

_____

_____

_____

_____

_____

_____

_____

_____

_____

_____

_____

_____

_____

_____

_____

Decimals

_____

_____

_____

_____

_____

_____

_____

_____

_____

_____

_____

_____

_____

_____

_____

_____

_____

_____

_____

NAME _____ DATE _____

7–18 FINDING THE 10s

Using the variables below, identify the expressions that equal 10.

> a = the number of wheels of a bicycle
> b = the number of singers in a trio
> c = four units to the left of zero
> d = the number of sides of a pentagon
> e = the number of wonders of the world
> f = the number of arms of an octopus

1. $ab - c =$ _____

2. $a + f + c + e =$ _____

3. $bc - a =$ _____

4. $\frac{1}{2} cd =$ _____

5. $-ad(b + c) =$ _____

6. $\frac{bd + e}{a} =$ _____

7. $ae - (c - b) =$ _____

8. $d - f + 4a - c =$ _____

9. $\frac{-2cd}{a^2} =$ _____

10. $(4b - a) \div (d + c) =$ _____

11. $\frac{(c - a)}{b} - (d - a)^2 =$ _____

12. $\frac{-c}{a}(d) =$ _____

The numbers of the problems whose answers equal 10: _____

NAME _____ DATE _____

7-19 CODE CRACKING

Choose the correct number or symbol from each pair to make each statement true. Then write the letters of your answers in order at the bottom of the sheet, starting with the first blank. When you are done, break the code by deciphering the words.

1. 45% of 92 = _____   **T.** 4.140 *or* **U.** 41.4

2. (87 − 23) − _____ = 25   **O.** 39 *or* **H.** 89

3. $\frac{5}{6} = \frac{\quad}{24}$ **Y.** 20 *or* **I.** 15

4. _____ ÷ 40 = 0.2   **S.** 0.8 *or* **E.** 8

5. 6.3 × _____ = 37.17   **I.** 0.59 *or* **R.** 5.9

6. $5\frac{3}{5} ÷$ _____ $= 1\frac{1}{5}$ **A.** $4\frac{2}{3}$ *or* **T.** $2\frac{3}{4}$

7. 3.528 _____ 3.5219   **L.** > *or* **E.** <

8. $\frac{1}{2} ÷ \frac{1}{2} =$ _____   **T.** $\frac{1}{4}$ *or* **U.** 1

9. 0.7 = _____   **H.** 7% *or* **F.** 70%

10. 72 ÷ 4 × 8 × 0 × 3 = _____   **E.** 432 *or* **S.** 0

11. 7 : 11 = _____   **S.** $\frac{7}{11}$ *or* **A.** $\frac{11}{7}$

12. _____ $- \frac{1}{4} = \frac{5}{12}$ **U.** $\frac{6}{16}$ *or* **E.** $\frac{2}{3}$

13. 9.4 = _____   **C.** $\frac{47}{5}$ *or* **M.** $\frac{18}{5}$

14. 23 × 100 = _____   **I.** 123 *or* **C.** 2,300

15. _____ ÷ 4 = $2\frac{1}{4}$ **R.** 10 *or* **U.** 9

16. 9.3 − _____ = 0.42   **S.** 8.88 *or* **B.** 9.58

__ __ __   __ __ __   __ __ __ __ __ __ __ __ __ __

NAME _____ DATE _____

7-20 TURNING IT AROUND

Follow the directions step by step. Give the coordinates of the arrow upon completion of step 7.

    1. Copy the arrow exactly as shown on a piece of graph paper.

    2. Rotate the figure 90° counterclockwise about (2,3).

    3. Translate this arrow 5 units to the left.

    4. Reflect it over the x-axis.

    5. Reflect it over the y-axis.

    6. Translate it up 1 unit.

    7. Rotate it 90° counterclockwise about the origin.

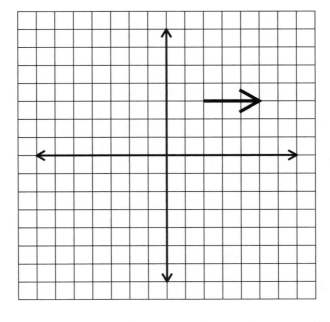

NAME _____   DATE _____

7-21   WHAT'S THE CONNECTION?

Place a check after the words or phrases in each set that are related to the given number. On the line below, write the relationship. The first one is done for you.

1. **100** =   dollar ✓   hour   century ✓
    _____ 100 cents in a dollar; 100 years in a century _____

2. **20** =   decade   score   fathom
    _____

3. **3** =   ZIP Code   area code   trio
    _____

4. **12** =   baker's dozen   knights   months
    _____

5. **7** =   Ages of Man   continents   oceans
    _____

6. **2** =   line   directions   double (baseball)
    _____

7. **4** =   quartet   seasons   square
    _____

8. **10** =   furlong   dozen   decade
    _____

9. **9** =   baseball   solar system   Wonders of the World
    _____

10. **1** =   millennium   whole   100%
    _____

NAME _____ DATE _____

7-22 TRACING NETWORKS

Several networks are shown below. Some can be traced without lifting your pencil from the paper and without writing over any segments or parts of any segment. You can write over points. Which networks can be traced?

1.

2.

3.

4.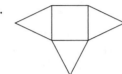

5.

6.

7.

8.

9.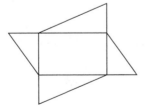

10.

Traceable networks: _____

NAME _____ DATE _____

7-23 VERY "PLANE"

Identify each vector and write its name after its component form. The first problem is done for you.

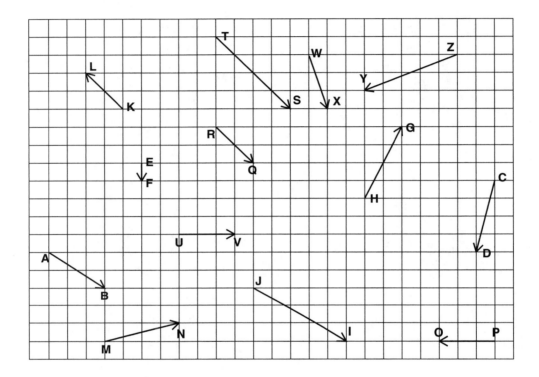

1. $\langle 2,4 \rangle$ $\overrightarrow{HG}$ 6. $\langle 3,0 \rangle$ _____   11. $\langle 3,-2 \rangle$ _____

2. $\langle 4,1 \rangle$ _____   7. $\langle -5,-2 \rangle$ _____   12. $\langle 2,-2 \rangle$ _____

3. $\langle 0,-1 \rangle$ _____   8. $\langle -3,0 \rangle$ _____   13. $\langle -1,-4 \rangle$ _____

4. $\langle 1,-3 \rangle$ _____   9. $\langle -2,2 \rangle$ _____

5. $\langle 4,-4 \rangle$ _____   10. $\langle 5,-3 \rangle$ _____

NAME _____   DATE _____

7–24 THE "BASES" OF THIS ACTIVITY

The numbers from 1 to 20 in Base 10 are listed on the left. Choose a number from the Answer Bank and match it with a number in Base 10. Each answer will be used only once.

Base 10	**Answer Bank**
1. _____	10,011 Base 2
2. _____	11 Base 2
3. _____	13 Base 8
4. _____	1,110 Base 2
5. _____	1,001 Base 2
6. _____	30 Base 5
7. _____	1 Base 5
8. _____	111 Base 2
9. _____	24 Base 8
10. _____	10 Base 5
11. _____	22 Base 8
12. _____	15 Base 8
13. _____	10,000 Base 2
14. _____	10 Base 8
15. _____	22 Base 5
16. _____	11 Base 5
17. _____	2 Base 5
18. _____	4 Base 8
19. _____	20 Base 5
20. _____	32 Base 5

NAME _____ DATE _____

7–25   SINES, COSINES, AND TANGENTS

A value, name of a trigonometric function, or angle is missing from each equation. Find what is missing.

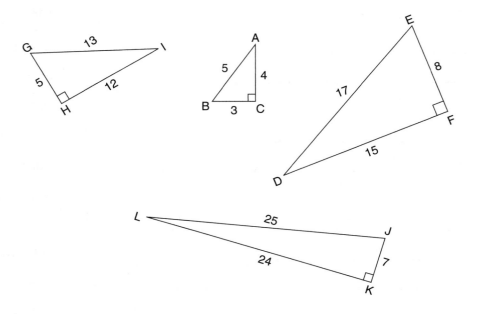

1. $\sin D = \dfrac{}{17}$

2. $\cos L = \dfrac{24}{}$

3. $\tan G = \dfrac{12}{}$

4. $\tan E = \dfrac{}{8}$

5. $\cos I = \dfrac{}{13}$

6. $\sin J = \dfrac{24}{}$

7. _____ $A = \dfrac{3}{4}$

8. _____ $E = \dfrac{15}{17}$

9. _____ $K = \phi$

10. _____ $B = \dfrac{3}{5}$

11. _____ $G = \dfrac{5}{13}$

12. _____ $L = \dfrac{7}{25}$

13. $\tan$ _____ $= 0.6$

14. $\tan$ _____ $= 1.875$

15. $\sin$ _____ $= 0.28$

16. $\cos$ _____ $= 0.8$

NAME _____   DATE _____

7–26   CONES, CONES, CONES

Graphs of conic sections may be represented in various forms. Match each equation with the appropriate figure listed in the Answer Bank.

$$a, b, > 0; \ (h,k) \text{ is the center}$$

1. $(x-h)^2 + (y-k)^2 = r^2$

2. $\dfrac{x^2}{a^2} + \dfrac{y^2}{b^2} = 1$

_____   _____

3. $y = ax^2$

4. $\dfrac{(x-h)^2}{a^2} - \dfrac{(y-k)^2}{b^2} = 1$

_____   _____

5. $x = ay^2$

6. $\dfrac{(x-h)^2}{a^2} + \dfrac{(y-k)^2}{b^2} = 1$

_____   _____

7. $(x-h)^2 + (y-k)^2 = r^2$

8. $y = ax^2 + bx + c$

_____   _____

9. $\dfrac{x^2}{a^2} - \dfrac{y^2}{b^2} = 1$

10. $\dfrac{(y-k)^2}{b^2} - \dfrac{(x-h)^2}{a^2} = 1$

_____   _____

11. $x = ay^2 + by + c$

12. $\dfrac{y^2}{b^2} - \dfrac{x^2}{a^2} = 1$

_____   _____

Answer Bank

circle   ellipse   parabola   hyperbola

NAME _____ DATE _____

7–27 NOT JUST FOR TECHIES

The following words relate to computers or the Internet. They are words you should know. Unscramble the words by using the clues.

1. **ekopdst:** primary display screen _____
2. **romemy:** storage area _____
3. **MOR:** type of memory designed to store low-level programs _____
4. **kocieo:** can also be a dessert or snack _____
5. **dewrahar:** computer and devices that connect to it _____
6. **enloni:** working on the Internet _____
7. **otob:** also can be worn on hikes _____
8. **etisbew:** interrelated webpages _____
9. **rachs:** a bad accident _____
10. **coin:** a picture _____
11. **pgramor:** also a TV show _____
12. **srucor:** it blinks _____
13. **rivus:** can cause an illness _____
14. **okarkbom:** a marker _____
15. **ARM:** also an animal _____
16. **il-ema:** not "snail mail" _____
17. **ptplao:** portable _____
18. **oumes:** also a varmint _____
19. **yteb:** used to represent numbers and letters _____
20. **srwopasd:** also the name of a quiz show and game _____
21. **ervesr:** also a waiter or waitress _____
22. **srobewr:** software that searches the World Wide Web _____
23. **gub:** also an insect _____
24. **UCP:** a computer's "brain" _____
25. **asworeft:** computer programs _____
26. **ciph:** a small piece _____
27. **dlodoawn:** to copy from the Internet _____
28. **pehomage:** main page of a website _____
29. **ncerhg saneie:** program that searches for information on the Web _____
30. **COM-DR:** type of compact disc _____

Copyright © 2004 by Judith A. Muschla and Gary Robert Muschla

Answer Key

Section 1

Worksheet 1–1   There's a Place for Everything
1. 641; 4   **2.** 75; 7   **3.** 23,568; 3   **4.** 31,239; 2   **5.** 19; 9   **6.** 2,517; 5   **7.** 350,794; 9
8. 261; 6   **9.** 17,064; 7   **10.** 183,610; 0   **11.** 315,980; 1   **12.** 199; 1   **13.** 18; 8
14. 56,092; 5   **15.** 3,654; 3

Worksheet 1–2   Finding Missing Numbers
1. 37; 22; 26; 3   **2.** 217; 922; 21; 630   **3.** 347; 1,348; 31; 5

Worksheet 1–3   Finding the Largest and Smallest
Approaches to setting up the problems may vary; possible approaches follow.
1. $96 + 83 = 179$ **2.** $983 + 64 = 1,047$ **3.** $94 - 86 = 8$ **4.** $234 - 98 = 136$
5. $94 \times 86 = 8,084$ **6.** $943 \times 86 = 81,098$ **7.** $24 \times 36 = 864$ **8.** $368 \times 24 = 8,832$
9. $9\overline{)234}$ (26)   **10.** $2\overline{)986}$ (493)

Worksheet 1–4   A Number Chain
1. 26   **2.** 76   **3.** Both numbers are the same.   **4.** The final answer is 1 less than the original number.

Worksheet 1–5   Which Is Greater?
Note: For easy recognition, the larger answer is indicated with a check. **1.** 7,565; 7,568✓
2. 17,784; 20,234✓   **3.** 4,764; 4,790✓   **4.** 1,003; 1,023✓   **5.** 971✓; 825   **6.** 216✓; 196
7. 3,204; 3,536✓   **8.** 227✓; 219   **9.** 85✓; 84   **10.** 560; 593✓   **11.** 1,510   **12.** 37,700   **13.** 25

Worksheet 1–6   The Trio Rounds to . . .
1. 15, 24, and 18 can be rounded to 20.   **2.** 158, 175, and 151 can be rounded to 200.
3. 12, 9, and 8 can be rounded to 10.   **4.** 254, 284, and 309 can be rounded to 300.
5. 991, 985, and 989 can be rounded to 1,000.   **6.** 550, 1,358, and 1,059 can be rounded
to 1,000.   **7.** 750, 801, and 843 can be rounded to 800.   **8.** 3,481, 3,505, and 3,516 can be
rounded to 3,500.   **9.** 1,850, 2,459, and 1,999 can be rounded to 2,000.   **10.** 2,497, 2,479,
and 2,515 can be rounded to 2,500.

Worksheet 1–7   A Fact About You
1. Y, 1   **2.** O, 2   **3.** U, 8   **4.** C, 12   **5.** A, 100   **6.** N, 101   **7.** F, 49   **8.** A, 100   **9.** C, 12
10. T, 90   **11.** O, 2   **12.** R, 36.   **Spells:** YOU CAN FACTOR.

Worksheet 1–8   Who Am I?
1. 7   **2.** 11   **3.** 1   **4.** 2   **5.** 97   **6.** 53   **7.** 0   **8.** 5   **9.** 6   **10.** 9   **11.** 101   **12.** 99

Worksheet 1–9   Which One Does Not Belong?
Note: Answers may vary; possible answers are shown. **1.** 7 is the only odd number; replace
with 12.   **2.** 9 is the only composite number; replace with 11.   **3.** 12 is the only number
that has a factor of 6; replace with 11.   **4.** 4 is not a multiple of 3; replace with 12.

5. 2 is the only prime number; replace with 4.   **6.** 20 is the only number that has a factor of 10; replace with 25.   **7.** 20 is the only number that is not a perfect square; replace with 36. **8.** 1313 is the only number that is not a palindrome; replace with 414.   **9.** 47 is the only number that doesn't start with a *th-* sound; replace with 37 or any number that starts with a *th-* sound.   **10.** 32 is the only number that is not the last day of a month; replace with 29 for February in a leap year.

Worksheet 1–10   Cross-Number Puzzle: Whole Numbers

1	3	4			1	2	8
	0					8	
	3	0	4		7	3	8
		9	7	1		8	
			3				
	1		8	9	8		
5	2	8	7		5	2	7	1
	4				0		
8	0	0		9	8	8	

Worksheet 1–11   The Powers of Prime
1. 5^2 **2.** 2^3 **3.** 3^3 **4.** 2^5 **5.** 7^2 **6.** 5^3 **7.** 2^2 **8.** 3^2 **9.** 7^3 **10.** 3^5 **11.** 11^2 **12.** 2^{11}

Worksheet 1–12   Cubes and Squares
1. 1   **2.** 64   **3.** 729   **4.** 26   **5.** 25   **6.** 100   **7.** 9   **8.** 16   **9.** 91   **10.** 24

Worksheet 1–13   An Exponential Typo
1. $2^3 + 74 = 82$ **2.** $92 - (3 + 6)^2 = 11$ **3.** $2^4 \div 2^3 = 2$ **4.** $(3 + 5)^2 - 6^2 - 7 \times 2^2 = 0$ **5.** $5^2 = 1^6 + 24$
6. $2^3 \div 4 = 2^1$ **7.** $2^4 = 6 \times 2^2 - 2^3$ **8.** $36 + 8^2 = 10^2$ **9.** $3^2 = 2^0 + 2^3$ **10.** $42 + 36 - 7^0 = 77$

Worksheet 1–14   Euclid and the GCF
1. 3   **2.** 1   **3.** 12   **4.** 2   **5.** 1   **6.** 3   **7.** 2   **8.** 3   **9.** 5   **10.** 1

Worksheet 1–15   Finding the LCM Using the GCF
1. 720   **2.** 1,032   **3.** 630   **4.** 1,728   **5.** 1,860   **6.** 2,728   **7.** 1,323   **8.** 874   **9.** 11,340
10. 2,688

Worksheet 1–16   The Missing Symbols
1. $8 \times 2 - 6 \div 3 = 14$ **2.** $3 \times 2 \times 6 - 4 = 32$ **3.** $16 \div 4 + 6 \times 1 = 10$ **4.** $9 - 8 + 3 \times 2 = 7$
5. $3(3 - 2) \div 3 = 1$ **6.** $12 - 3 \times 2 \times 2 = 0$ **7.** $(7 \times 4 - 1) \div 3 = 9$ **8.** $(1 + 8) \div (6 + 3) = 1$
9. $15 \div 5 \times 3 - 7 = 2$ **10.** $(15 - 3) \div 4 + 8 = 11$

Worksheet 1–17   What a Mix-Up!
1. 9   **2.** 7   **3.** 4   **4.** 5   **5.** 2   **6.** 10   **7.** 6   **8.** 1   **9.** 3   **10.** 8

Worksheet 1–18   A Perfect 10

Answers may vary; possible answers are shown. **1.** $2 \times 6 \div (4 + 8) = 1$ **2.** $8 \div 2 + 4 - 6 = 2$
3. $(6 + 8) \div 2 - 4 = 3$ **4.** $4 \div 2 + 8 - 6 = 4$ **5.** $4 \times 6 \div 8 + 2 = 5$ **6.** $6 + 8 - 2 \times 4 = 6$
7. $2(6 + 8) \div 4 = 7$ **8.** $6 + 8 - (2 + 4) = 8$ **9.** $(2 + 4) \div 6 + 8 = 9$ **10.** $6 \times 8 \div 4 - 2 = 10$

Worksheet 1–19   Not-So-Famous Firsts for Presidents

1. 5   **2.** 25   **3.** 18   **4.** 13   **5.** 3   **6.** 14   **7.** 26   **8.** 77   **9.** 36   **10.** 41   **11.** 6   **12.** 16

Worksheet 1–20   What's Next?

Answers may vary; possible answers follow.

1. 5, 6, 7, 8, 9, 10; add 1 to the previous number.   **2.** 1, 2, 4, 8, 16, 32; multiply previous number by 2.   **3.** 9, 8, 7, 6, 5, 4; subtract 1 from the previous number.   **4.** 0, 5, 10, 15, 20, 25; add 5 to the previous number.   **5.** 2, 3, 5, 7, 11, 13; prime numbers.   **6.** 1, 4, 9, 16, 25, 36; square numbers.   **7.** 9, 12, 15, 18, 21, 24; add 3 to the previous number.
8. 480, 240, 120, 60, 30, 15; divide previous number by 2.   **9.** 2, 5, 11, 23, 47, 95; multiply the previous number by 2 and add 1.   **10.** 4, 5, 7, 10, 14, 19; add 1, then 2, then 3, etc., to each successive previous number.

Worksheet 1–21   Numbers of All Kinds

1. composite   **2.** factors   **3.** even   **4.** figurate   **5.** abundant   **6.** prime   **7.** multiples
8. odd   **9.** palindrome   **10.** whole   **11.** perfect   **12.** deficient   **13.** emirp   **14.** cardinal
15. natural

Worksheet 1–22   Val's Baby-sitting Job

8, $24, 15, $21, $3, $36, $57

Worksheet 1–23   Is the Price Right?

1. $11 (consonants cost $5; vowels cost $1)   **2.** $13 (consonants cost $2; vowels cost $3)
3. $10 (consonants cost $4; vowels cost $1)   **4.** $12 (consonants cost $2; vowels cost $1)
5. $13 (consonants cost $3; vowels cost $4)

Section 2

Worksheet 2–1   Fractional Trivia

1. $\frac{9}{24}$ **2.** $\frac{2}{4}$ **3.** $\frac{42}{54}$ **4.** $\frac{3}{5}$ **5.** $\frac{54}{63}$ **6.** $\frac{35}{60}$ **7.** $\frac{10}{14}$ **8.** $\frac{156}{195}$ **9.** $\frac{6}{9}$ **10.** $\frac{294}{336}$ **11.** $\frac{3}{12}$ **12.** $\frac{208}{286}$

Worksheet 2–2   Odd Fraction Out

1. $\frac{6}{8}$; $\frac{6}{10}$ **2.** $\frac{7}{8}$; $\frac{20}{30}$ **3.** $\frac{12}{90}$; $\frac{10}{45}$ **4.** $\frac{28}{30}$; $\frac{8}{10}$ **5.** $\frac{14}{18}$; $\frac{42}{48}$ **6.** $\frac{12}{27}$; $\frac{12}{28}$ **7.** $\frac{25}{36}$; $\frac{55}{66}$ **8.** $\frac{9}{15}$; $\frac{18}{24}$
9. $\frac{49}{121}$; $\frac{49}{77}$ **10.** $\frac{10}{60}$; $\frac{60}{144}$

Worksheet 2–3   Don't Be Redundant

1. 0.875   **2.** correct   **3.** $0.\overline{5}$ **4.** $0.1\overline{6}$ **5.** $0.\overline{27}$ **6.** $0.\overline{714285}$ **7.** correct   **8.** correct
9. $0.\overline{15}$ **10.** $0.\overline{148}$ **11.** correct   **12.** $0.8\overline{3}$ **13.** correct   **14.** $0.2\overline{7}$ **15.** 0.0625

Worksheet 2–4   Out of Order

1. $\frac{7}{25}, \frac{3}{10}, \frac{7}{20}, \frac{9}{25}$ **2.** $\frac{1}{3}, \frac{2}{5}, \frac{1}{2}, \frac{3}{4}$ **3.** $\frac{4}{5}, \frac{7}{8}, \frac{8}{9}, \frac{9}{10}$ **4.** $\frac{1}{4}, \frac{19}{50}, \frac{49}{100}, \frac{1}{2}$ **5.** $\frac{5}{7}, \frac{3}{4}, \frac{4}{5}, \frac{8}{9}$
6. $\frac{1}{3}, \frac{3}{8}, \frac{4}{9}, \frac{4}{7}$ **7.** $\frac{5}{8}, \frac{11}{15}, \frac{3}{4}, \frac{7}{9}$ **8.** $\frac{1}{5}, \frac{2}{9}, \frac{3}{11}, \frac{5}{13}$ **9.** $\frac{4}{9}, \frac{5}{11}, \frac{3}{5}, \frac{7}{8}$ **10.** $\frac{2}{3}, \frac{4}{5}, \frac{9}{11}, \frac{7}{8}$

Worksheet 2–5   Don't Be Square

12	24	2	30
18	14	28	8
32	4	22	10
6	26	16	20

Worksheet 2–6   Boxes and Numbers

1. $\frac{2}{8} + \frac{4}{6} = \frac{11}{12}$ **2.** $\frac{2}{6} + \frac{4}{8} = \frac{5}{6}$ **3.** $\frac{4}{6} - \frac{2}{8} = \frac{5}{12}$ **4.** $\frac{4}{8} - \frac{2}{6} = \frac{1}{6}$ **5.** $\frac{2}{4} \times \frac{6}{8} = \frac{3}{8}$

6. $\frac{2}{6} \times \frac{4}{8}$ or $\frac{2}{8} \times \frac{4}{6} = \frac{1}{6}$ **7.** $\frac{2}{4} \div \frac{6}{8}$ or $\frac{2}{6} \div \frac{4}{8} = \frac{2}{3}$ **8.** $\frac{2}{8} \div \frac{4}{6} = \frac{3}{8}$

Worksheet 2–7   Think About This

Answers may vary; possible answers are shown. **1.** $\frac{1}{2}, \frac{1}{3}$ **2.** $\frac{1}{3}, \frac{1}{4}$ **3.** $\frac{1}{1}$ **4.** $\frac{1}{1}, \frac{1}{2}$ **5.** $\frac{2}{3}$

6. $\frac{5}{8}, \frac{8}{5}$ **7.** $\frac{1}{2}, \frac{1}{3}$ **8.** $1\frac{2}{5}, 1\frac{1}{4}$ **9.** $\frac{1}{4}, \frac{1}{3}, \frac{1}{5}$ **10.** $\frac{1}{7}, \frac{2}{7}, \frac{4}{7}$

Worksheet 2–8   Filling in Fractions

1. $5\frac{2}{4} + 3\frac{6}{8} = 9\frac{1}{4}$ **2.** $7\frac{3}{6} - 4\frac{2}{8} = 3\frac{1}{4}$ **3.** $3\frac{2}{8} - 1\frac{4}{6} = 1\frac{7}{12}$ **4.** $3\frac{4}{6} \times 1\frac{2}{8} = 4\frac{7}{12}$

5. $2\frac{4}{8} \div 6 = \frac{5}{12}$ **6.** $6\frac{2}{4} \div 8\frac{1}{3} = \frac{39}{50}$

Worksheet 2–9   Making a Match

1. Y, $\frac{11}{3}$ **2.** O, $1\frac{1}{4}$ **3.** U, $3\frac{11}{24}$ **4.** A, $1\frac{2}{9}$ **5.** R, $4\frac{3}{8}$ **6.** E, $1\frac{2}{3}$ **7.** C, $2\frac{5}{9}$ **8.** O, $1\frac{1}{4}$

9. R, $4\frac{3}{8}$ **10.** R, $4\frac{3}{8}$ **11.** E, $1\frac{2}{3}$ **12.** C, $2\frac{5}{9}$ **13.** T, $1\frac{7}{12}$ **Spells:** YOU ARE CORRECT.

Worksheet 2–10   Not Really Complex at All

1. $1\frac{1}{2}$ **2.** $1\frac{1}{9}$ **3.** 6   **4.** 14   **5.** $\frac{1}{10}$ **6.** $8\frac{1}{4}$ **7.** $1\frac{37}{88}$ **8.** $2\frac{5}{14}$ **9.** $1\frac{7}{8}$ **10.** $\frac{7}{9}$ **11.** $1\frac{1}{3}$ **12.** $2\frac{1}{5}$

Worksheet 2–11   Making a Point

1. 16.398   **2.** 3.7268   **3.** 95.146   **4.** 8.7143   **5.** 385.79   **6.** 724.68   **7.** 9,253.7   **8.** 6.71845
9. 59,423.7   **10.** 59.3148   **11.** 92,346.8   **12.** 463,749.5   **13.** 45,286.05   **14.** 64.31298
15. 0.5398712

Worksheet 2–12   More or Less

1. $0.\overline{3} < 0.5$ **2.** $0.1\overline{6} < 0.25$ **3.** $0.1\overline{6} = 0.1\overline{6}$ **4.** $0.8 > 0.75$ **5.** $0.25 = 0.25$ **6.** $0.25 < 0.\overline{3}$
7. $0.\overline{6} = 0.\overline{6}$ **8.** $0.5 = 0.5$ **9.** $0.15 < 1.5$ **10.** $0.125 < 0.25$ **11.** $0.58\overline{3} < 0.8\overline{3}$ **12.** $0.25 > 0.1\overline{6}$

Worksheet 2–13   What Comes First?

1. 0.13 baseball cards (1900)   **2.** 0.1352 Ping-Pong (1901)   **3.** 0.136 Teddy bear (1902)
4. 0.52 jigsaw puzzles (1909)   **5.** 0.6 Raggedy Ann doll (1918)   **6.** 1 miniature golf
(1926)   **7.** 1.3 Yo-Yo (1929)   **8.** 1.36 Monopoly (1933)   **9.** 1.632 Scrabble (1943)

10. 1.74 Silly Putty (1944)   **11.** 2.14 Frisbee (1957)   **12.** 2.403 Barbie doll (1959)   **13.** 2.41 Easy Bake Oven (1963)   **14.** 5.0 G.I. Joe (1964)   **15.** 5.8 skateboards (1975)   **16.** 5.81 Cabbage Patch Kids doll (1983)   **17.** 5.8102 Teenage Mutant Ninja Turtles (1989)   **18.** 5.83 Rollerblades (1990)   **19.** 6.08 Beanie Babies (1994)   **20.** 6.8 Tickle Me Elmo (1996)

Worksheet 2–14   What's the Point?

1. $\frac{7}{2}$ **2.** $\frac{3}{4}$ **3.** $\frac{7}{4}$ **4.** $\frac{32}{9}$ **5.** $\frac{1}{3}$ **6.** $\frac{21}{10}$ **7.** $\frac{1}{2}$ **8.** $\frac{11}{10}$ **9.** $\frac{11}{5}$ **10.** $\frac{1}{9}$ **11.** $\frac{31}{8}$ **12.** $\frac{25}{8}$

13. $\frac{5}{3}$ **14.** $\frac{17}{6}$

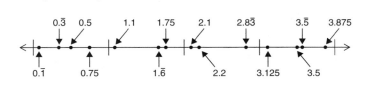

Worksheet 2–15   Decimal Round-Up

1. All except 0.35 can be rounded to 0.3.   **2.** All except 0.333 can be rounded to 0.32.
3. All except 8.41 can be rounded to 9.   **4.** All except 37.152 can be rounded to 38.
5. All except 150.45 can be rounded to 150.4.   **6.** All except 1.375 can be rounded to 1.3.   **7.** All except 1.84 can be rounded to 1.9.   **8.** All except 15.285 can be rounded to 15.4.   **9.** All except $\frac{5}{6}$ can be rounded to 0.   **10.** All except $3\frac{7}{8}$ can be rounded to 3.4.

Worksheet 2–16   A Decimal Cross Number Puzzle

4	8	. 6			1	5	. 4	
	. 2					2		
	6	3	. 7		1	. 2	6	
		2	1	. 5		. 2		
		2						
	3		5	. 7	9			
1	. 4	7	6		2	3	. 7	8
	0					1		
8	5	. 4			3	4	. 7	

Worksheet 2–17   The Missing Link

1. 4   **2.** 53.75   **3.** 2.68   **4.** 36   **5.** 4.958   **6.** 0.9   **7.** 7.2   **8.** 0.7   **9.** 4.5   **10.** 5.86

Worksheet 2–18   Get the Point

1. $45.2 - 3.75 = 41.45$ **2.** $0.962 \times 2.5 = 2.405$ **3.** $7.56 \div 0.32 = 23.625$
4. $6.8 + 24.5 = 31.3$ **5.** $0.56 \div 0.025 = 22.4$ **6.** $469 - 213.2 = 255.8$ **7.** $0.002 \times 123 = 0.246$
8. $2.4 \div 1.2 + 7.02 = 9.02$ **9.** $7.5 + 3.45 - 0.23 = 10.72$ **10.** $1.64 \div 4.0 \times 38.2 = 15.662$

Worksheet 2–19   At the Mall

1. $15.99   **2.** $1.97   **3.** $11.98   **4.** $0.59   **5.** 3 for $1.95   **6.** $5.70   **7.** $3.47   **8.** $11.99

Worksheet 2–20   Do You Have Some Change?
These answers can be in any order. **1.** $6.98   **2.** $6.94   **3.** $6.89   **4.** $6.74   **5.** $6.90
6. $6.85   **7.** $6.70   **8.** $6.80   **9.** $6.65   **10.** $6.50

Worksheet 2–21   Human Body Statistics
1. 2.4×10^9 **2.** 7.5×10^{13}; 2×10^9 **3.** 1.5×10^0; 8.75×10^{-1} **4.** 6×10^4 **5.** 6×10^2; 1×10^3
6. 1×10^{-1}; 2×10^{-1} **7.** 3×10^{-1}; 7×10^{-1} **8.** 2.23×10^2

Worksheet 2–22   Celestial Facts
1. 36,000,000 miles   **2.** 92,960,000 miles   **3.** 240,000 miles   **4.** 3,666,000,000 miles
5. 27,000,000° F   **6.** 8,700° F   **7.** 430,000 miles   **8.** 186,000 miles per second

Worksheet 2–23   Right and Wrong
1. $1\frac{3}{8}, \frac{5}{14}, 1\frac{3}{8}$ **2.** $\frac{27}{40}, \frac{27}{40}, \frac{5}{8}$ **3.** $4\frac{5}{18}, 4\frac{5}{18}, 4\frac{1}{6}$ **4.** $1\frac{33}{100}, 1\frac{7}{8}, 1\frac{7}{8}$ **5.** 0.45, 4.5, 0.45
6. 8.4, 8.75, 8.75   **7.** 4.4, 4.4, 4.3   **8.** 1.122, 1.2, 1.122

Worksheet 2–24   Mystery Ratios
1. 4 : 5   **2.** 1 : 1   **3.** 3 : 2   **4.** 9 : 1   **5.** 1 : 1   **6.** 1 : 3   **7.** 6 : 5   **8.** 256 : 63   **9.** 6 : 11
10. 4 : 3

Worksheet 2–25   How Do You Rate?
1. 1 : 5   **2.** 2 : 3   **3.** 1 : 5   **4.** 4 : 1   **5.** 1 : 500   **6.** 1 : 4   **7.** 1 : 12   **8.** 1 : 12   **9.** 1 : 1
10. 1 : 2   **11.** 2 : 1   **12.** 1 : 4   **13.** 3 : 1   **14.** 1 : 4   **15.** 1 : 1

Worksheet 2–26   What's Cooking?
1. $\frac{3}{4}$ cup   **2.** $\frac{3}{4}$ slice   **3.** $2\frac{1}{2}$ cups   **4.** $1\frac{1}{2}$ cups   **5.** $\frac{1}{3}$ pound   **6.** $9\frac{1}{3}$ crackers   **7.** $17\frac{1}{2}$ cups
8. $1\frac{1}{5}$ cups

Worksheet 2–27   Finding the Third
1. 50%   **2.** $0.8\overline{3}$ **3.** $\frac{4}{5}$ **4.** 0.75   **5.** $33\frac{1}{3}$%   **6.** $0.\overline{5}$ **7.** 30%   **8.** $\frac{1}{4}$ **9.** $\frac{2}{3}$ **10.** 20%
11. $\frac{1}{8}$ **12.** 0.0625   **13.** 37.5%   **14.** 0.9   **15.** $\frac{1}{6}$ **16.** 0.7

Worksheet 2–28   Times Change
1. 13.5   **2.** 55%   **3.** 90   **4.** 18   **5.** 87.5%   **6.** 80   **7.** 119   **8.** 50   **9.** 140   **10.** 450%

Worksheet 2–29   Percents with a Twist
1. 112.5   **2.** 20   **3.** 20%   **4.** 160   **5.** 40   **6.** 31.25%   **7.** 130   **8.** $88.\overline{8}$%

Worksheet 2–30   Short Work of Percents
1. T   **2.** H   **3.** E   **4.** S   **5.** E   **6.** A   **7.** R   **8.** E   **9.** A   **10.** L   **11.** L   **12.** R   **13.** I
14. G   **15.** H   **16.** T   **Spells:** THESE ARE ALL RIGHT.

Section 3

Worksheet 3–1   What's the Angle?
1. 90°   **2.** 75°   **3.** 55°   **4.** 90°   **5.** 130°   **6.** 105°   **7.** 60°   **8.** 60°   **9.** 40°   **10.** 110°
11. 91°   **12.** 89°

Worksheet 3–2   Quilting Lines

$\overline{AB} \parallel \overline{IJ} \parallel \overline{LK} \parallel \overline{DC}$

$\overline{AD} \parallel \overline{IL} \parallel \overline{JK} \parallel \overline{BC}$

$\overline{EF} \parallel \overline{MN} \parallel \overline{OP} \parallel \overline{GH} \parallel \overline{DL} \parallel \overline{JB}$

$\overline{FG} \parallel \overline{NO} \parallel \overline{MP} \parallel \overline{EH} \parallel \overline{AI} \parallel \overline{KC}$

$\overline{AD} \perp \overline{DC}$	$\overline{AI} \perp \overline{EF}$	$\overline{EF} \perp \overline{FG}$
$\overline{DC} \perp \overline{BC}$	$\overline{JB} \perp \overline{FG}$	$\overline{FG} \perp \overline{GH}$
$\overline{BC} \perp \overline{AB}$	$\overline{KC} \perp \overline{HG}$	$\overline{GH} \perp \overline{EH}$
$\overline{AD} \perp \overline{AB}$	$\overline{EH} \perp \overline{LD}$	$\overline{EF} \perp \overline{EH}$

$\overline{IJ} \perp \overline{JK}$	$\overline{MN} \perp \overline{NO}$
$\overline{JK} \perp \overline{LK}$	$\overline{NO} \perp \overline{OP}$
$\overline{IL} \perp \overline{LK}$	$\overline{OP} \perp \overline{MP}$
$\overline{IL} \perp \overline{JI}$	$\overline{MP} \perp \overline{MN}$

Worksheet 3–3   Counting Sides
1. 19   **2.** 5   **3.** 12   **4.** 10   **5.** 16   **6.** 3   **7.** 9   **8.** 20   **9.** 6   **10.** 17   **11.** 11   **12.** 4   **13.** 18
14. 13   **15.** 7   **16.** 15   **17.** 8   **18.** 14

Worksheet 3–4   Sometimes It's Right!
1. 60°, acute   **2.** 30°, acute   **3.** 90°, right   **4.** 110°, obtuse   **5.** 90°, right   **6.** 20°, acute
7. 10°, obtuse   **8.** 50°, right   **9.** 40°, acute.   All missing measures are multiples of 10.

Worksheet 3–5   Find the Right Word
equilateral; two; scalene; all; complementary; three; obtuse; acute; sixty; isosceles; no; interior

Worksheet 3–6   What's My Line?
$\overline{ED}$ is the perpendicular bisector. $\overline{CD}$ is a median. $\overline{AF}$ is an altitude. $\overline{BG}$ is an angle bisector.

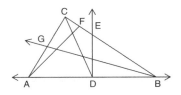

Worksheet 3–7   Angles and Measures

Worksheet 3–7   Angles and Measures

$m\angle 2 = m\angle 4 = m\angle 6 = m\angle 8 = m\angle 16 = m\angle 18 = 70°$

$m\angle 1 = m\angle 3 = m\angle 5 = m\angle 7 = m\angle 17 = m\angle 19 = 110°$

$m\angle 14 = m\angle 24 = 30°$

$m\angle 12 = m\angle 10 = m\angle 20 = m\angle 22 = 80°$

$m\angle 9 = 30°$

$m\angle 11 = m\angle 13 = m\angle 21 = m\angle 23 = 100°$

$m\angle 15 = m\angle 25 = 150°$

Worksheet 3–8   A Quadrilateral by Any Other Name

1. quadrilateral, parallelogram, rectangle, rhombus, square   **2.** quadrilateral, trapezoid
3. quadrilateral, parallelogram   **4.** quadrilateral, parallelogram, rhombus   **5.** quadrilateral, parallelogram, rectangle   **6.** quadrilateral

Worksheet 3–9   What's the Measure?

1. $m\angle A = m\angle C = 60°$; $m\angle B = 120°$ **2.** $m\angle A = m\angle B = m\angle C = m\angle D = 90°$ **3.** $m\angle A = m\angle B = 90°$; $m\angle C = 130°$ **4.** $m\angle A = m\angle C = 80°$; $m\angle B = 100°$ **5.** $m\angle B = 115°$; $m\angle D = 90°$ **6.** $m\angle A = 120°$; $m\angle B = 85°$ **7.** $m\angle D = 109°$; $m\angle A = m\angle C = 71°$ **8.** $m\angle A = m\angle B = m\angle C = m\angle D = 90°$
9. $m\angle A = m\angle C = 55°$; $m\angle B = m\angle D = 125°$

Worksheet 3–10   A Polygon Word Find

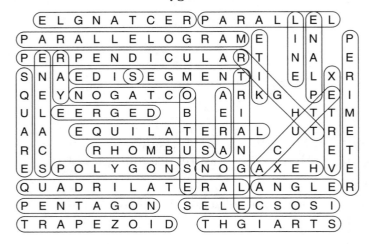

Worksheet 3–11   Always, Sometimes, Never

1. always   **2.** sometimes   **3.** never   **4.** always   **5.** sometimes   **6.** always   **7.** never
8. never   **9.** always   **10.** sometimes   **11.** sometimes   **12.** never   **13.** sometimes
14. sometimes   **15.** sometimes

Worksheet 3–12   Different and Yet the Same

1. All are complementary angles.   **2.** All are acute angles.   **3.** All are angles of a triangle.
4. All are equilateral triangles.   **5.** All are isosceles triangles.   **6.** All are trapezoids.
7. All have a perimeter of 16.   **8.** All are rectangles.   **9.** All are parallelograms.   **10.** All are regular polygons.

Worksheet 3–13   What's the Relationship?

1. $m\angle A = 81°$; $m\angle D = 81°$; $m\angle B = 27°$ **2.** $m\angle C = 90°$; $m\angle B = 75°$ **3.** $m\angle A = 56.25°$;
$m\angle C = 33.75°$; $m\angle B = 18.75°$ **4.** $m\angle A = 135°$; $m\angle B = 45°$ **5.** $m\angle A = 76.5°$; $m\angle B = 25.5°$;

$m\angle D = 78°$ **6.** $m\angle A = 136\frac{2}{7}°$; $m\angle B = 45\frac{3}{7}°$; $m\angle C = 60\frac{3}{7}°$; $m\angle D = 117\frac{6}{7}°$ **7.** $m\angle C = 45.75°$; $m\angle D = 88.5°$; $m\angle B = 30.75°$ **8.** $m\angle A = 90°$; $m\angle B = 30°$

Worksheet 3–14   All, Some, or No

1. All **2.** Some **3.** Some **4.** Some **5.** No **6.** Some **7.** All **8.** Some **9.** All **10.** All

Worksheet 3–15   Finding the Proof

Answers may vary; possible answers follow. **1.** $\overline{AB} \cong \overline{DE}$; $\overline{BC} \cong \overline{EF}$; $\overline{AC} \cong \overline{DF}$ **2.** $\overline{AB} \cong \overline{DE}$; $\overline{AC} \cong \overline{DF}$ **3.** $\angle C \cong \angle F$; $\overline{BC} \cong \overline{EF}$ **4.** $\overline{AC} \cong \overline{DF}$; $\angle C \cong \angle F$ **5.** $\overline{HI} \cong \overline{LJ}$; $\overline{GI} \cong \overline{KJ}$ **6.** $\overline{GH} \cong \overline{KL}$; $\overline{GI} \cong \overline{KJ}$ **7.** $\angle H \cong \angle L$; $\overline{HI} \cong \overline{LJ}$ **8.** $\angle H \cong \angle L$; $\overline{GH} \cong \overline{KL}$ **9.** $\overline{MN} \cong \overline{QP}$; $\overline{NO} \cong \overline{PO}$; $\overline{MO} \cong \overline{QO}$ **10.** $\overline{NO} \cong \overline{PO}$; $\overline{MO} \cong \overline{QO}$ **11.** $\overline{NO} \cong \overline{PO}$ **12.** $\overline{MN} \cong \overline{QP}$

Worksheet 3–16   Finding Right Triangles

Problems 1, 2, 5, 7, and 10 are right triangles. **3.** Change 33 to 40. **4.** Change 11 to 12. **6.** Change 37 to 36. **8.** Change 89 to 99. **9.** Change 57 to 60.

Worksheet 3–17   Figure This

1. 15; $45° - 45° - 90°$ **2.** 2; $30° - 60° - 90°$ **3.** $2\sqrt{5}$; $30° - 60° - 90°$ **4.** $5\sqrt{2}$; $45° - 45° - 90°$ **5.** $\sqrt{3}$; $45° - 45° - 90°$; **6.** $\sqrt{6}$; $30° - 60° - 90°$; **7.** $6\sqrt{2}$; $30° - 60° - 90°$; **8.** $2\sqrt{2}$; $45° - 45° - 90°$; **9.** $10\sqrt{15}$; $30° - 60° - 90°$; **10.** $\sqrt{10}$; $45° - 45° - 90°$

Worksheet 3–18   Picture This

Students must draw the following: **1.** any angle **2.** any two intersecting lines **3.** an isosceles triangle **4.** an equilateral triangle **5.** a parallelogram that is not a rectangle or rhombus **6.** an isosceles trapezoid **7.** a rectangle that is not a square **8.** a square **9.** a pentagon with 2 pairs of congruent sides and a base that has a different length **10.** a regular pentagon

Worksheet 3–19   Spinning Around

1. both **2.** line symmetry **3.** both **4.** rotational symmetry **5.** line symmetry **6.** neither **7.** both **8.** line symmetry **9.** both **10.** both **11.** rotational symmetry **12.** line symmetry

Worksheet 3–20   Don't Go in Circles!

1. arc **2.** center **3.** chord **4.** semicircle **5.** pi **6.** circle graph **7.** degrees **8.** radius **9.** concentric circles **10.** wheel **11.** sphere **12.** diameter **13.** rings **14.** compact disc **15.** circumference

Worksheet 3–21   A Circle Word Find

Worksheet 3–22   Complete the Circle
1. center   2. radii   3. isosceles   4. 50   5. 65   6. diameter   7. chord   8. 130   9. semicircle   10. secant line   11. 90   12. right triangle   13. minor   14. major   15. tangent line   16. right   17. supplementary   18. acute   19. complementary   20. exterior

Worksheet 3–23   A Circular Chain
1. $x = 8$ 2. $y = 10$ 3. $z = 10$ 4. $a = 21$ 5. $b = 42$

Worksheet 3–24   3-D Word Scramble
1. cube   2. sphere   3. cone   4. base   5. vertex   6. cylinder   7. pyramid   8. face
9. prism   10. dice   11. edge   12. circle   13. tube   14. soda can   15. rectangle
16. altitude

Worksheet 3–25   Finding 3-D Figures
1. cube   2. cylinder   3. rectangular prism   4. cone   5. diameter of a sphere   6. edge
7. polyhedra or polyhedrons   8. hemisphere   9. net   10. regular polyhedron
11. pyramid   12. vertex

Worksheet 3–26   A Great Swiss Mathematician
1. 6   2. 6   3. 12   4. 12   5. 12   6. 60   7. 5   8. 8   9. 6   10. 6

Section 4

Worksheet 4–1   Going to Great Lengths
1. 4 inches by 6 inches   2. 36 inches   3. 1 inch   4. 9 inches by 2 inches   5. $4\frac{5}{6}$ feet
6. 1,328 miles   7. 1,092 miles   8. 5 by 6 feet   9. 70 feet   10. 4 inches; 1 inch
11. 2,056 feet   12. 2.28 miles

Worksheet 4–2   The Long and Short of It
1. 2.67 decimeters   2. 77 millimeters by 126 millimeters   3. 2.3 centimeters
4. 305 millimeters   5. 1.42 decimeters   6. 1,000 millimeters   7. 0.91 meters
8. 24.5 centimeters   9. 48.26 centimeters   10. 155.58 millimeters   11. 2.22 centimeters
12. 0.733 meters   13. 3,931.62 kilometers   14. 1,585.85 kilometers   15. 6,697.6 kilometers
16. 8,848.03 meters

Worksheet 4–3   Going the Distance
1. 1.5   2. $1\frac{1}{4}$ 3. $1\frac{3}{4}$ 4. 4   5. 10   6. 45   7. $3\frac{3}{8}$ 8. $\frac{1}{4}$ 9. 1.15   10. $\frac{3}{4}$
F is the midpoint of $\overline{DG}$ and $\overline{CH}$. E is the midpoint of $\overline{AH}$.

Worksheet 4–4   Not Just for Cooking
1. 2   2. 4   3. 8   4. 16   5. 48   6. 2   7. 16   8. 4   9. 32   10. 8   11. 16   12. 128

Worksheet 4–5   Odd Measure Cut
1. 24 inches   2. 6 cups   3. 0.5 pounds   4. 0.1 mile   5. 18 fluid ounces   6. 1.3 feet
7. 20 fluid ounces   8. 500 pounds   9. 4 cups   10. 0.25 pounds   11. 4 fluid ounces
12. $\frac{1}{5}$ mile

Worksheet 4–6   Getting to the Basics
1. Kelvin   2. second   3. ampere   4. mole   5. meter   6. gram   7. candela

Worksheet 4–7   Equal or Not Equal

Correct: problems 2, 4, 8, and 10. **1.** Replace 100 m with 1,000 m.   **3.** Replace 150,000 dg with 15,000 dg.   **5.** Replace 15.5 hg with 155 hg.   **6.** Replace 0.15 m with 0.015 m. **7.** Replace 1.2 mm with 120 mm.   **9.** Replace 35 L with 0.0035 L.

Worksheet 4–8   It's About Time

Answers may vary; possible answers follow. **1.** Susan worked from 9:00 A.M. to 5:30 P.M. How many hours was she actually paid?   **2.** If Susan starts work at 9:00 A.M., what time should she leave for work?   **3.** How much will Susan earn if she works a forty-hour week? **4.** How much will Susan earn if she works forty-five hours for one week?   **5.** If Susan works from noon to 6:00 P.M., what time should she leave her home, and what time should she arrive home?   **6.** If Susan worked from 9:00 A.M. to 5:30 P.M., how many hours did she actually work?

Worksheet 4–9   Never Enough Time

1. $6.40   **2.** 1:25   **3.** 85   **4.** 2:20 P.M.   **5.** 90   **6.** 2002, 2112   **7.** 4:15 P.M.   **8.** 46 hours

Worksheet 4–10   Timely Words

1. fortnight   **2.** biennium   **3.** score   **4.** millennium   **5.** annual   **6.** biannual **7.** biweekly   **8.** semiannual   **9.** quadrennial   **10.** centennial   **11.** bicentennial **12.** tricentennial

Worksheet 4–11   Coded Equations

1. 12 inches in a foot   **2.** 100 cents in a dollar   **3.** 90 feet between bases in baseball **4.** 4 quarts in a gallon   **5.** 4 quarters in a dollar   **6.** 90 degrees in a right angle **7.** 20 years in a score   **8.** 144 items in a gross   **9.** 500 sheets of paper in a ream **10.** X equals ten in Roman numerals   **11.** 4 seasons in a year   **12.** 24 hours in a day **13.** 186,282 miles per second equals the speed of light   **14.** 2 times a radius equals a diameter   **15.** 144 square inches in a square foot

Worksheet 4–12   How Do You Measure Up?

Answers may vary; possible answers follow. **1.** 2 pints = 1 quart   **2.** 3 feet = 1 yard **3.** 4 quarts = 1 gallon   **4.** 7 days = 1 week   **5.** 8 fluid ounces = 1 cup   **6.** 9 square feet = 1 square yard   **7.** 10 years = 1 decade   **8.** 12 months = 1 year   **9.** 16 ounces = 1 pound **10.** 24 hours = 1 day   **11.** 36 inches = 1 yard   **12.** 60 minutes = 1 hour   **13.** 90° = 1 right angle   **14.** 100 years = 1 century   **15.** 144 square inches = 1 square foot   **16.** 180° = a straight angle   **17.** 360° = a circle   **18.** 1,760 yards = 1 mile   **19.** 2,000 pounds = 1 ton **20.** 5,280 feet = 1 mile.

Worksheet 4–13   Take Your Measure

1. gross   **2.** decibel   **3.** bolt   **4.** acre   **5.** horsepower   **6.** ream   **7.** ampere   **8.** knot **9.** dozen   **10.** ohm   **11.** chain   **12.** light-year   **13.** astronomical unit   **14.** karat **15.** score   **16.** hand   **17.** bale   **18.** hertz   **19.** barometer   **20.** parsec

Worksheet 4–14   Matching Temperatures

1. 190° C   **2.** 113° F   **3.** –5° C   **4.** 0° C   **5.** 104° F   **6.** 37° C   **7.** 212° F   **8.** 44.6° F **9.** 80° C   **10.** 95° F

Worksheet 4–15   A Matter of Degree

1. A. 70°   **2.** P. 50°   **3.** R. 40°   **4.** O. 130°   **5.** T. 90°   **6.** R. 40°   **7.** A. 70°   **8.** C. 150° **9.** T. 90°   **10.** O. 130°   **11.** R. 40°   **Spells:** A PROTRACTOR.

Worksheet 4–16   A Slice of the Circle
1. $\frac{\pi}{6}$ 2. $45°$ 3. $\frac{\pi}{3}$ 4. $75°$ 5. $\frac{\pi}{2}$ 6. $\frac{7\pi}{12}$ 7. $120°$ 8. $135°$ 9. $\frac{5\pi}{6}$ 10. $165°$
11. $180°$ 12. $\frac{7\pi}{6}$ 13. $240°$ 14. $\frac{3\pi}{2}$ 15. $\frac{5\pi}{3}$ 16. $360°$

Worksheet 4–17   Finding the Way Around
1. $x = 18$ cm   2. $x = 21$ cm   3. $x = 2$ ft.; $y = 3$ ft.; $z = 5$ ft.   4. $x = 6$ in.; $y = 28$ in.   5. $x = 4$ in.
6. $x = 25$ cm

Worksheet 4–18   Going Around in "Squares"
The last figure in the third row has a perimeter of 10 units. The others have a
perimeter of 12 units.

Worksheet 4–19   Sketching It Out
1. 25 square inches   2. 74 inches; 40 inches; 30 inches; 26 inches; 24 inches   3. 2 units
by 8 units; 4 units by 4 units   4. 40 inches   5. 20 units   6. 144 square inches; 48 inches

Worksheet 4–20   Different Figures, Same Areas
1. $w = 4$; $h = 3$ 2. $h = 14$; $b = 4$ 3. $l = 10$; $h = 3$ 4. $s = 8$; $b_2 = 20$ 5. $h = 10$; $w = 7$
6. $d = 16$; $r = 8$

Worksheet 4–21   Drawing Geometric Figures
Answers may vary; possible shapes follow. **1.** a 4 by 4 square and a 2 by 8 rectangle
2. a right triangle whose legs are 3 units and 4 units, and an acute triangle whose height
is 3 units and base is 4 units   **3.** the same figures as problem 2 except that the triangle
should be obtuse rather than acute   **4.** a 4 by 8 rectangle and a 1 by 11 rectangle
5. a 4 by 5 rectangle and a parallelogram whose base is 5 and height is 4   **6.** a square
divided along its diagonal, forming two congruent triangles   **7.** a square divided at the
midpoints of the opposite sides, forming two congruent rectangles

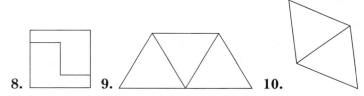

8.   9.   10.

Worksheet 4–22   All Related
1. 45 square units   2. 64 square units   3. 24 square units   4. 240 square units
5. 36 square units   6. 336 square units   7. 24 square units   8. 24 square units

Worksheet 4–23   Going Full Circle
1. 78.5 square units   2. 31.4 units   3. $315°$ 4. $90°$ 5. 3.925 units   6. 11.775 units
7. $60°$ 8. $5.2\overline{3}$ units   9. $22.8958\overline{3}$ square units   10. $26.1\overline{6}$ square units   11. 29.4375
square units   12. The sum of the areas of the sectors is the same as the area of the circle.

Worksheet 4–24   Know What Formula to Use
1. I   2. A   3. E   4. G   5. C   6. L or J   7. J   8. F   9. B   10. H   11. K   12. D

Worksheet 4–25   Formulas to the Max
1. D   2. G, A, B, H   3. B, H, C, F   4. E   5. F   6. F   7. B, H

Worksheet 4–26   A Step Beyond
1. 96; 64   **2.** 5; 150   **3.** 7; 343   **4.** 280; 300   **5.** 8; 312   **6.** 6; 120   **7.** 36; 12   **8.** 2; 120

Worksheet 4–27   Same and Different
1. Figures 1 and 2; $V = 64$ cubic units   **2.** Figures 1 and 3; $SA = 76$ square units   **3.** Figures 1 and 3; $V \approx 56.52$ cubic units   **4.** Figures 2 and 3; $V = 40.5$ cubic units   **5.** Figures 1 and 2; $SA \approx 452.16$ square units

Worksheet 4–28   What's the Value?
1. $w = 2$ **2.** $h = 15$ **3.** $r = 1$ **4.** $h = \frac{4}{3}$ **5.** $h = 3$ **6.** $s = \sqrt{15}$ **7.** $s = 2\frac{2}{3}$ **8.** $r = 3$ **9.** $r = \sqrt{10}$

Worksheet 4–29   Double Trouble
1. doubled; 4   **2.** twice; 2   **3.** doubled, doubled; 4   **4.** doubled; 4   **5.** 8, 4   **6.** 8

Worksheet 4–30   Measuring Up
1. T; 1 mile = 63,360 inches; 1 ton = 32,000 ounces   **2.** F; 1,440 minutes in a day; 14,400 seconds in 4 hours   **3.** F; 8,800 yards in 5 miles; 13,200 feet in 2.5 miles   **4.** T; 144 square inches in a square foot; 90 square feet in 10 square yards   **5.** T; 16 fluid ounces in a pint; 8 pints in a gallon   **6.** F; 1,296 square inches in a square yard; 46,656 cubic inches in a cubic yard   **7.** F; 16 tablespoons in a cup; 128 fluid ounces in a gallon   **8.** F; 880 yards in half a mile; 2,420 square yards in half an acre   **9.** T; 240 inches in 20 feet; 180 degrees between the freezing and boiling point on the Fahrenheit scale   **10.** F; 512 fluid ounces in 4 gallons; 640 acres in a square mile   **11.** T; 1,728 inches in a cubic foot; 180 inches in 5 yards (final answer: *barleycorns*)

Section 5

Worksheet 5–1   Finding Solutions
1. $a \times b$ **2.** $b - a$ **3.** $a \div b$ **4.** $a + b + c$ **5.** $c \div (a + b)$ **6.** $(a + b + c + d + e) \div 5$
7. Expression depends upon which is the larger sum; could be $(a + b) - (c + d)$ or $(c + d) - (a + b)$ **8.** $2(a + b)$

Worksheet 5–2   According to the Facts
1. 45   **2.** 27   **3.** 39   **4.** 29   **5.** 29   **6.** 30   **7.** 36   **8.** 86   **9.** 20; 11   **10.** 23; 26
11. 35; 27   **12.** $16,000; $11,000   **13.** 10; 16   **14.** 165; 235   **15.** 53   **16.** 12; 29
17. 25; 30; 60   **18.** 63; 71; 94

Worksheet 5–3   A Sweet Time Line
In order on the number line: Hershey's Bar, 1894; Cracker Jack, 1896; Hershey's Kisses, 1907; M&M's, 1920; Baby Ruth, 1921; Milky Way, 1923; Snickers, 1930; 3 Musketeers, 1932; Almond Joy, 1947; Reese's Pieces, 1978

Worksheet 5–4   A Place for Everything

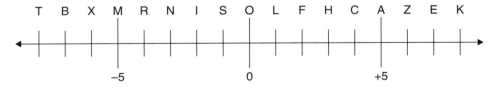

Worksheet 5–5 Finding the Expressions

1. $3 - (-3) = 5 + 1$ **2.** $-2 - 6 = -10 + 2$ **3.** $-7 + 3 = -2 + (-2)$ **4.** $-8 - (-2) = 5 - 11$
5. $-15 + (-2) = 20 + (-37)$ **6.** $-3 - 4 + (-5) = -6 + (-6)$ **7.** $-9 - (-3) - (-10) = 12 + (-8)$
8. $-10 - (-2) + 13 = -8 - (-6) + 7$ **9.** $-2 + (-3) + 5 = -2 + 4 + 8 - 10$ **10.** $-3 + 8 - (-4) =$
$7 - 1 + 3$ **11.** $-2 + 3 - (-5) = 8 - (-2) - 4$ **12.** $-13 - (-3) - (-6) = 8 + -5 + -10 - (-3)$

Worksheet 5–6 Counting Down

1. $-5 \times (-2)$ **2.** $-3 \times (-3)$ **3.** $-16 \div (-2)$ **4.** $-49 \div (-7)$ **5.** $-3 \times (-2)$ **6.** $-20 \div (-4)$
7. $-28 \div (-7)$ **8.** $9 \div 3$ **9.** $44 \div 22$ **10.** $-18 \div (-18)$ **11.** $0 \div (-10)$ **12.** $8 \div (-8)$
13. $-26 \div 13$ **14.** -1×3 **15.** -2×2 **16.** $-35 \div 7$ **17.** -3×2 **18.** $7 \times (-1)$ **19.** -4×2
20. $-36 \div 4$ **21.** $50 \div (-5)$

Worksheet 5–7 Finding the Largest and Smallest

1. $9 + 8 = 17$ **2.** $9 - (-6) = 15$ **3.** $9 \times 8 = 72$ **4.** $-6 \div (-3) = 2$ **5.** $-3 + (-6) = -9$
6. $-6 - 9 = -15$ **7.** $-6 \times 9 = -54$ **8.** $9 \div (-3) = -3$ (The sum of the answer is 25.)

Worksheet 5–8 Integer Facts

1. always **2.** always **3.** never **4.** always **5.** never **6.** sometimes **7.** sometimes
8. never **9.** never **10.** sometimes **11.** always **12.** sometimes

Worksheet 5–9 Parentheses, Please

1. $8 - (4 + (-3)) = 7$ **2.** $3((-4) + 2) = -6$ **3.** $18 \div ((-11) + 2) = -2$ **4.** $-9 \times 4 \div ((-1) - 2)$
$= 12$ **5.** $(-3 + 5) \div (-2) = -1$ **6.** $-8 \div (4 - 2) \times 6 = -24$ **7.** $(32 - 8) \times (-4) = -96$
8. $-36 \times (4 - 4) = 0$ **9.** $(14 + (-1) + (-7)) \div 3 = 2$ **10.** $4 + 10 \div ((-6) - 4) = 3$
11. $16 \div (8 - 4) = 4$ **12.** $(6 + 3) \times (-2) = -18$

Worksheet 5–10 Numbers in Boxes

1. $\frac{-1}{-2} + \frac{3}{4} = 1\frac{1}{4}$ **2.** $\frac{-2}{3} - \frac{-1}{6} = -\frac{1}{2}$ **3.** $\frac{-2}{3} \times \frac{-1}{4} = \frac{1}{6}$ **4.** $\frac{3}{4} \div \frac{-1}{6} = -4\frac{1}{2}$
5. $-2\frac{5}{6} - \frac{-1}{3} = -2\frac{1}{2}$ **6.** $4\frac{3}{5} \times \frac{-2}{-1} = 9\frac{1}{5}$

Worksheet 5–11 Putting the Fun in Functions

1. $k(7)$ **2.** $g(-1)$ **3.** $f(0)$ **4.** $k(5)$ **5.** $f(6)$ **6.** $k(-2)$ **7.** $f(4)$ **8.** $f(-3)$ **9.** $g(2)$ **10.** $h(1)$
11. $g(6)$ **12.** $k(-5)$ **13.** $f(2) + h(2)$ **14.** $k(-3) - h(-3)$ **15.** $k(-4) - f(-4)$ **16.** $g(-6) - h(-6)$

Worksheet 5–12 Finding the Fourth

1. $(20,21)$; $y = x + 1$ **2.** $(7,49)$; $y = x^2$ **3.** $(20,40)$; $y = 2x$ **4.** $(-5,-6)$; $y = x - 1$ **5.** $(-10, -13)$;
$y = x - 3$ **6.** $(-6,-15)$; $y = 2x - 3$ **7.** $(-5,26)$; $y = x^2 + 1$ **8.** $(5,16)$; $y = 3x + 1$ **9.** $(-10,5)$;
$y = x \div (-2)$ **10.** $(-4,64)$; $y = (2x)^2$

Worksheet 5–13 Absolutely Sure!

1. 4 **2.** 6 **3.** 10 **4.** -7 **5.** 15 **6.** 1 **7.** 12 **8.** 8 **9.** -19 **10.** -6 **11.** -9 **12.** -30
13. -10 **14.** 0 **15.** 5

Worksheet 5–14 The Lucky 13

1. $4b = 0$ **2.** $af = -6$ **3.** $a + c = 2$ **4.** $d - e = -16$ **5.** $c(d - a) = 9$ **6.** $a \times d = -18$
7. $a \times d \times f = 36$ **8.** $\frac{c \times d}{a} = 2$ **9.** $f^a = -8$ **10.** $c^a = -1$ **11.** $a = d \div f$ **12.** $e \div f = d - c$
13. $a - d = e - c$

Worksheet 5–15   An Equation Chain
1. $a = 5$ **2.** $b = 11$ **3.** $c = 4$ **4.** $d = 12$ **5.** $e = 7$ **6.** $f = 14$ **7.** $g = 4$ **8.** $h = 2$ **9.** $i = 3$
10. $j = 7$ **11.** $k = 14$ **12.** $l = 12$ **13.** $m = 10$ **14.** $a = 5$

Worksheet 5–16   Matching Equations
1 and 6 $x = 10.6$;   **2 and 3** $x = 3.8$;   **4 and 13** $x = -2.55$;   **5 and 14** $x = -6$;   **7 and 11** $x = -14$;
8 and 17 $x = 24$;   **9 and 12** $x = -10$;   **10 and 15** $x = -18$;   **16 and 18** $x = -0.5$

Worksheet 5–17   Not Quite Right
1. correct   **2.** $x = 0$ **3.** $x = -8$ **4.** correct   **5.** correct   **6.** $x = -\frac{1}{3}$ **7.** correct   **8.** $x = 5$
9. $x = \frac{11}{15}$ **10.** correct

Worksheet 5–18   Correct Solutions
1. $3(x + 7) = 27$ **2.** $(2x)^2 = 36$ **3.** $3 - (x + 4) = -8$ **4.** $1 = (x + 1)^0$ **5.** $15 \div (x - 3) = 3$
6. $(x + 4) \div (x - 20) = -5$ **7.** $2 + x - (3x + 1) = 11$ **8.** $3x + 3 = 3(x + 1)$
9. $2(x + 4(x + 1)) = 18$ **10.** $3x \div (x - 1) = \phi$

Worksheet 5–19   Get to the Point!
1. $(0,0)$ **2.** points on the y-axis   **3.** points on the x-axis   **4.** points in the first quadrant
5. points in the second and fourth quadrants   **6.** points on the line $y = x$ **7.** points in the
second and fourth quadrants   **8.** points on the line $y = 5$ **9.** points on the line $y = -x$
10. $(0,0)$

Worksheet 5–20   Common Knowledge
1. All are written in slope intercept form.   **2.** All lines go through the origin.   **3.** All have
a positive slope.   **4.** All are horizontal lines and have a slope = 0.   **5.** All are equations of
the same line.   **6.** All stand for slope.   **7.** All have the same y-intercept.   **8.** All points are
on the y-axis.   **9.** All points are in the third quadrant.   **10.** All points are 2 units from the
origin.

Worksheet 5–21   A Shining Star
1. $x = -2$; $y = -4$ **2.** $x = 5$; $y = 1$ **3.** $x = -4$; $y = 1$ **4.** $x = 2$; $y = -4$ **5.** $x = 1$; $y = 4$

Worksheet 5–22   Doubletalk
1. $(4,2)$ **2.** $(3,7)$ **3.** $(-3,3)$ **4.** $(0,1)$ **5.** $(2,1)$ **6.** $(0,7)$ **7.** $(-1,5)$ **8.** $(5,-2)$
9. $(-2,-3)$ **10.** $(4,-1)$

Worksheet 5–23   A Radical Change
1. $4\sqrt{2}$ **2.** $3\sqrt{2}$ **3.** 4 **4.** $2\sqrt{6}$ **5.** $2\sqrt{30}$ **6.** $2\sqrt{3}$ **7.** 12 **8.** $2\sqrt{7}$ **9.** $7\sqrt{2}$ **10.** $5\sqrt{6}$

Worksheet 5–24   Radical Matches
1 and 13 $5\sqrt{2}$;   **2 and 17** $\sqrt{6}$;   **3 and 11** $4\sqrt{3}$;   **4 and 19** $5\sqrt{3}$;   **5 and 15** $\sqrt{6} + 2\sqrt{3}$;
6 and 14 $4\sqrt{5}$;   **7 and 20** $2\sqrt{2} + 2\sqrt{3}$;   **8 and 18** $\sqrt{2}$;   **9 and 12** $8\sqrt{3}$;   **10 and 16** $5\sqrt{5}$;

Worksheet 5–25   All in the Range
1. $x = \pm 10$ **2.** $x = 8$ and $x = -6$ **3.** $x = 0$ and $x = -6$ **4.** $x = \pm 4$ **5.** $x = \pm 5$ **6.** $x = 0$ and $x = \frac{-4}{3}$
7. $x = \frac{-13}{24}$ and $x = \frac{-19}{24}$ **8.** $x = 10$ and $x = 0$ **9.** $x = 2$ and $x = -1$ **10.** $x = \pm \frac{3}{2}$

Worksheet 5–26   And the Answer Is . . .
1. 1 **2.** 3; -5 **3.** 4 **4.** -2; $\frac{1}{2}$ **5.** $\sqrt{3}$; $-\sqrt{3}$ **6.** $\frac{1 + \sqrt{13}}{2}$; $\frac{1 - \sqrt{13}}{2}$ **7.** $\frac{-3 + \sqrt{21}}{2}$; $\frac{-3 - \sqrt{21}}{2}$
8. $-1, -3$ **9.** $\frac{-5}{2}$; $\frac{5}{2}$ **10.** $\frac{-3}{2}$; $\frac{4}{3}$

Worksheet 5–27   Varying Values
1. $b = 7$; $a = 1$; $c = 5$ or $b = 7$; $a = 5$, $c = 1$ **2.** $b = -6$; $a = 1$; $c = 9$ or $b = -6$, $a = 9$, $c = 1$
3. $b = -1$; $a = 4$; $c = 5$ or $b = -1$, $c = 4$, $a = 5$ **4.** $b = -20$; $a = 4$; $c = 25$ or $b = -20$, $c = 25$,
$a = 4$ **5.** $b = 4$; $a = 1$, $c = 3$ or $b = 4$, $a = 3$, $c = 1$ **6.** $b = 0$; $a = 1$; $c = 4$ or $b = 0$; $a = 4$; $c = 1$

Worksheet 5–28   Common to Both
1. 3   **2.** x **3.** $2x$ **4.** $x + 4$ **5.** $x + 9$ **6.** $x + 3$ **7.** $x - 2$ **8.** $3x + 1$ **9.** $4x - 3$ **10.** $2x - 4$

Worksheet 5–29   Something's Wrong
The incorrect problems and their solutions follow: **Problem 2.** $x < 2$ **Problem 3.** $x \geq 3$
Problem 4. $x > -4$ **Problem 6.** $x > 5$ **Problem 7.** $x \geq 10$ **Problem 9.** $x > 3$
Problem 11. $x \geq -2$

Worksheet 5–30   Absolutely Correct
1. $x = 7$ or $x = -7$ **2.** ϕ **3.** $x < 6$ and $x > -6$ **4.** $x \geq 8$ or $x \leq -8$ **5.** $x = 5$, $x = -5$
6. $x = 6$, $x = -14$ **7.** $x \leq 15$ and $x \geq -5$ **8.** $x < -1$ and $x > -17$ **9.** $x > 3$ or $x < -9$
10. $x = 4$, $x = -4\frac{2}{3}$ **11.** $x > -4\frac{1}{2}$ and $x < 5\frac{1}{2}$ **12.** $x > 2\frac{1}{3}$ or $x < -5$

Worksheet 5–31   Find the Function
1. $f(x) = x^2$ **2.** $f(x) = x - 7$ **3.** $f(x) = x$
   $g(x) = x + 2$ $g(x) = \sqrt{x}$ $g(x) = x - 7$

4. $f(x) = x - 1$ **5.** $f(x) = x^2$ **6.** $f(x) = x - 1$
   $g(x) = x^2 - 1$ $g(x) = x - 1$ $g(x) = 2x$

Worksheet 5–32   Relativity
1. $y = x^2$ **2.** $y = x^2$; $y = |x|$; $y = \sqrt{x}$ **3.** $y = [|x|]$ **4.** $y = x^2$; $y = |x|$ **5.** $y = x$; $y = \frac{1}{x}$ **6.** $y = x$;
$y = x^3$; $y = \frac{1}{x}$ **7.** $y = x$; $y = x^3$ **8.** $y = \frac{1}{x}$ **9.** $y = x^2$; $y = \mathrm{x}^3$; $y = \frac{1}{x}$; $y = \sqrt{x}$ **10.** $y = \sqrt{x}$

Worksheet 5–33   Just Passing Through
1. I, III   **2.** III, IV   **3.** I, II   **4.** II, IV   **5.** I, II, III   **6.** I   **7.** I, III   **8.** I, II, IV   **9.** I, II
10. I, III, IV   **11.** I, II   **12.** I, II, III   **13.** II, III, IV   **14.** I, III   **15.** I, II, III, IV   **16.** IV

Worksheet 5–34   Defining Expressions
2. all real numbers except 0   **4.** all real numbers except –8   **7.** all real numbers greater
than 0   **8.** all real numbers greater than or equal to –3   **9.** all real numbers except 0
11. all real numbers except 2 and –2   **13.** all real numbers greater than or equal to 8
14. all real numbers except 8   **15.** all real numbers except 2 and 5

Worksheet 5–35   How Well Do You Function?
1. h **2.** g **3.** h **4.** h; $x \neq 3$ **5.** f **6.** h **7.** k **8.** g; $x \neq 3$; $x \neq 1$ **9.** f, k **10.** g, k **11.** g; k
12. k; h; $x \neq 1$; $x \neq -1$

Section 6

Worksheet 6–1   Passing the Test
1. D   **2.** C   **3.** A   **4.** F   **5.** B   **6.** E

Worksheet 6–2   Inserting the Missing Data
1. 82   **2.** 93   **3.** 70   **4.** 82   **5.** 93   **6.** 85   **7.** 84   **8.** 87

Worksheet 6–3   Charting the Temperatures

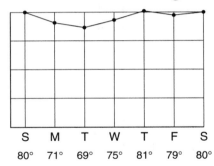

S	M	T	W	T	F	S
80°	71°	69°	75°	81°	79°	80°

Worksheet 6–4   A Piece of the Pie

clothing $80; gasoline $40; entertainment $80; food $60; taxes $40; phone $60; miscellaneous expenses $40

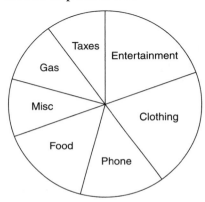

Worksheet 6–5   Mark That Date

1. A, $\frac{1}{2}$ **2.** R, $\frac{9}{28}$ **3.** E, $\frac{3}{28}$ **4.** C, $\frac{1}{14}$ **5.** O, $\frac{5}{28}$ **6.** R, $\frac{9}{28}$ **7.** R, $\frac{9}{28}$ **8.** E, $\frac{3}{28}$ **9.** C, $\frac{1}{14}$
10. T, $\frac{1}{7}$ **11.** I, $\frac{1}{28}$ **12.** S, $\frac{2}{7}$ **13.** O, $\frac{5}{28}$ **14.** N, $\frac{19}{28}$ **15.** E, $\frac{3}{28}$ (The probability that all your answers ARE CORRECT IS ONE.)

Worksheet 6–6   All About Data

1. bar graph   **2.** pie graph   **3.** pictograph   **4.** scattergram   **5.** frequency table   **6.** trend line   **7.** stem-and-leaf plot   **8.** histogram   **9.** line graph   **10.** box-and-whisker plot

Worksheet 6–7   A Matrix Chain

1. $C=\begin{bmatrix} 5 & -3 & 9 \\ 8 & 8 & -2 \end{bmatrix}$ **2.** $E=\begin{bmatrix} 4 & -7 & 7 \\ -2 & 4 & -1 \end{bmatrix}$ **3.** $G=\begin{bmatrix} 2 & -3 & -1 \\ 5 & 5 & 2 \end{bmatrix}$ **4.** $I=\begin{bmatrix} -1 & -1 & 3 \\ -1 & 5 & -1 \end{bmatrix}$

5. $K=\begin{bmatrix} 2 & -3 & 4 \\ 6 & 1 & 2 \end{bmatrix}$ Matrix A and matrix K are equal.

Worksheet 6–8   The Missing Elements

1. $\begin{bmatrix} 12 & 9 \\ -6 & 18 \end{bmatrix}$ **2.** $[27]$ **3.** $\begin{bmatrix} -13 \\ 29 \end{bmatrix}$ **4.** $\begin{bmatrix} -21 & 1 \\ 7 & -9 \end{bmatrix}$ **5.** $\begin{bmatrix} 23 & -11 \\ -20 & 26 \\ 19 & -17 \end{bmatrix}$

Worksheet 6–9   The Odds Are . . .

1. $\frac{1}{13}$, $\frac{1}{12}$ 2. $\frac{1}{10}$, $\frac{1}{9}$ 3. $\frac{2}{11}$, $\frac{2}{9}$ 4. $\frac{3}{10}$, $\frac{3}{7}$ 5. $\frac{1}{5}$, $\frac{1}{4}$ 6. $\frac{3}{5}$, $\frac{3}{2}$ 7. $\frac{1}{3}$, $\frac{1}{2}$ 8. $\frac{4}{13}$, $\frac{4}{9}$

9. $\frac{2}{5}$, $\frac{2}{3}$ 10. $\frac{2}{7}$, $\frac{2}{5}$

Section 7

Worksheet 7–1   Deuces Are Wild

Answers may vary; possible answers follow. $10 - 8 = 2$; $8 \div 4 = 2$; $4 + 5 - 7 = 2$;
$(8 + 6) \div 7 = 2$; $(4 + 5) \div 3 - 1 = 2$; $3 - (5 - 4) = 2$; $(9 \times 4) \div (3 \times 6) = 2$

Worksheet 7–2   Finding Missing Numbers

1. 84   **2.** 321   **3.** 25   **4.** 96   **5.** 243   **6.** 2   **7.** 11,140   **8.** 46   **9.** 320   **10.** 1,010

Worksheet 7–3   Make a Quiz

Reasonable quizzes are acceptable.

Worksheet 7–4   Reading the Signs

1. $4892 + 375 = 5{,}267$ **2.** $4074 \div 42 = 97$ **3.** $5274 \times 28 = 147{,}672$
4. $90052 - 4758 = 85{,}294$ **5.** $39153 \div 93 = 421$ **6.** $2795 + 8639 = 11{,}434$
7. $276 \times 457 = 126{,}132$ **8.** $53278 - 6953 = 46{,}325$ **9.** $9{,}678 \times 152 = 1{,}471{,}056$
10. $995{,}250 \div 375 = 2{,}654$

Worksheet 7–5   Wheeling Around

1.

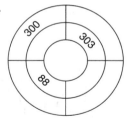

2.

3.

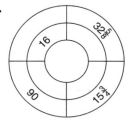

4.

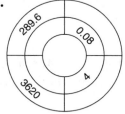

Worksheet 7–6   Math Tic-Tac-Toe

1.

×	×	
×	×	×

2.

×		×
		×
	×	×

3. Answers may vary.

Worksheet 7–7   It's a Date
1. 530 B.C.   **2.** 300 B.C.   **3.** 100   **4.** 200   **5.** 600   **6.** 1478   **7.** 1489   **8.** 1500   **9.** 1540
10. 1580   **11.** 1630   **12.** 1650   **13.** 1680   **14.** 1810   **15.** 1840   **16.** 1905   **17.** 1916
18. 1945   **19.** 1976   **20.** 1995

Worksheet 7–8   Left to Right or Right to Left
Answers may vary; possible answers follow. **1.** $32.41 + 13.13 = 45.54$ **2.** $937 - 301 = 636$
3. $11 \times 33 = 363$ **4.** $440 \div 8 = 55$ **5.** $\frac{7}{33} + \frac{4}{33} = \frac{11}{33}$ **6.** $848 \div 2 = 424$ **7.** A side = 11 units;
the area is 121 square units.   **8.** The sides are 15 units, 8 units, and 10 units. The perimeter is 33 units.

Worksheet 7–9   What's the Problem?
Answers may vary; reasonable problems are acceptable.

Worksheet 7–10   And the Question Is . . .
Answers may vary; reasonable problems are acceptable.

Worksheet 7–11   You're the Teacher
1. The student found the total bill, not the change.   **2.** The student wrote the ratio of
wins to the number of games played.   **3.** The student rounded the sales tax to $1.67
instead of $1.68.   **4.** The student did not change the feet to yards for the dimensions of
the room. He or she actually found the cost of carpeting a nine-yard-by-twelve-yard room.
5. The student multiplied the radius by two instead of squaring the radius.   **6.** The student
treated the two successive discounts as a reduction of 20%.   **7.** The student found the
number of inches in a foot.   **8.** The student divided by 2, not by 3.   **9.** The student
found the average of 40 and 60.   **10.** The student found the cost of six notebooks by
multiplying $6 \times \$1.50$ and then adding the other items.

Worksheet 7–12   Finding Missing Information
Answers may vary for some problems; possible answers follow. **1.** 14   **2.** 30; 15   **3.** $75;
$35   **4.** $65; $7.50   **5.** $29.99; $19.99

Worksheet 7–13   Create a Pattern
1. 9, 7, 5, 3, 1   **2.** $2\frac{1}{2}$, 3, $3\frac{1}{2}$, 4, $4\frac{1}{2}$ **3.** 100, 80, 60, 40, 20   **4.** 3.25, 2.75, 2.25, 1.75, 1.25
5. 5, 25, 125, 625, 3,125   **6.** 4, 4.25, 4.5, 4.75, 5   **7.** 80, 81, 83, 86, 90   **8.** 4, 9, 16, 25, 36
9. 42, 40, 36, 30, 22   **10.** 1, 0.1, 0.01, 0.001, 0.0001   **11.** $\frac{1}{2}$, $\frac{1}{3}$, $\frac{1}{4}$, $\frac{1}{5}$, $\frac{1}{6}$ **12.** $\frac{1}{2}$, $\frac{2}{3}$, $\frac{3}{4}$, $\frac{4}{5}$, $\frac{5}{6}$

Worksheet 7–14   Signs
1. $8 \times 4 - 3 = 29$ **2.** $24 \div 8 \times 5 = 15$ **3.** $9 \times 4 \div 6 = 6$ **4.** $(8 + 4) \div 3 = 4$ **5.** $9 + 7 - (2 \times 3)$
$= 10$ **6.** $(25 - 5) \div (3 + 1) = 5$ **7.** $7 \times 2 + 4 - 2 = 16$ **8.** $(4 \times 4) - (2 \times 8) = 0$ **9.** $6 \div 3 + 8$
$- 4 = 6$ **10.** $(12 - 6) \times (7 - 5) = 12$

Worksheet 7–15   Numbers and Values
1. 25%   **2.** 4 out of 5   **3.** $4^2 + 3$ **4.** $2^3 + 1$ **5.** $2^2 + 2^2$ **6.** $\frac{15}{2}$ **7.** $\frac{3}{10}$ **8.** $6\frac{3}{4}$ **9.** 100%
10. $\frac{1}{6}$ **11.** $2^2 + 3^2$ **12.** 0.05

Worksheet 7–16   A Mixed-up Magic Square

1	15	14	4
12	6	7	9
8	10	11	5
13	3	2	16

Magic number is 34.

Worksheet 7–17   Math Word Chains
Accept reasonable lists.

Worksheet 7–18   Finding the 10s
1. 10   **2.** 13   **3.** –14   **4.** –10   **5.** 10   **6.** 11   **7.** 21   **8.** 9   **9.** 10   **10.** 10   **11.** –11   **12.** 10
(The expressions that equal 10: numbers 1, 5, 9, 10, 12)

Worksheet 7–19   Code Cracking
1. U, 41.4   **2.** O. 39   **3.** Y, 20   **4.** E, 8   **5.** R, 5.9   **6.** A, $4\frac{2}{3}$ **7.** L, >   **8.** U, 1   **9.** F, 70%
10. S, 0   **11.** S, $\frac{7}{11}$ **12.** E, $\frac{2}{3}$ **13.** C, $\frac{47}{5}$ **14.** C, 2,300   **15.** U, 9   **16.** S, 8.88   **Spells:** YOU ARE SUCCESSFUL.

Worksheet 7–20   Turning It Around

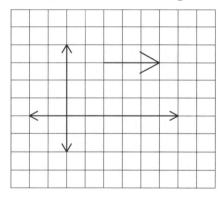

Worksheet 7–21   What's the Connection?
1. One hundred cents in a dollar; one hundred years in a century   **2.** Twenty years in a score   **3.** Three numbers in an area code; three singers in a trio   **4.** Twelve knights of Arthur's Round Table; twelve months in the year   **5.** Seven Ages of Man according to Shakespeare; seven continents (North America, South America, Europe, Africa, Asia, Australia, Antarctica)   **6.** Two points to a line; two bases in a double (baseball)   **7.** Four singers in a quartet; four seasons in the year; four angles, or four sides, in a square
8. Ten years in a decade   **9.** Nine innings in a regulation baseball game; nine planets in the solar system   **10.** One whole; 100% equals one whole

Worksheet 7–22   Tracing Networks

1, 2, 3, 4, 7, 9

Worksheet 7–23   Very "Plane"

1. $\overrightarrow{HG}$ 2. $\overrightarrow{MN}$ 3. $\overrightarrow{EF}$ 4. $\overrightarrow{WX}$ 5. $\overrightarrow{TS}$ 6. $\overrightarrow{UV}$ 7. $\overrightarrow{ZY}$ 8. $\overrightarrow{PO}$ 9. $\overrightarrow{KL}$ 10. $\overrightarrow{JI}$ 11. $\overrightarrow{AB}$
12. $\overrightarrow{RQ}$ 13. $\overrightarrow{CD}$

Worksheet 7–24   The "Bases" of This Activity

1. 1 Base 5   2. 2 Base 5   3. 11 Base 2   4. 4 Base 8   5. 10 Base 5   6. 11 Base 5   7. 111
Base 2   8. 10 Base 8   9. 1,001 Base 2   10. 20 Base 5   11. 13 Base 8   12. 22 Base 5
13. 15 Base 8   14. 1,110 Base 2   15. 30 Base 5   16. 10,000 Base 2   17. 32 Base 5
18. 22 Base 8   19. 10,011 Base 2   20. 24 Base 8

Worksheet 7–25   Sines, Cosines, and Tangents

1. 8   2. 25   3. 5   4. 15   5. 12   6. 25   7. tan   8. sin   9. tan   10. cos   11. cos   12. sin
13. *A*   14. *E*   15. *L*   16. *A*

Worksheet 7–26   Cones, Cones, Cones

1. circle   2. ellipse   3. parabola   4. hyperbola   5. parabola   6. ellipse   7. circle
8. parabola   9. hyperbola   10. hyperbola   11. parabola   12. hyperbola

Worksheet 7–27   Not Just for Techies

1. desktop   2. memory   3. ROM   4. cookie   5. hardware   6. online   7. boot
8. website   9. crash   10. icon   11. program   12. cursor   13. virus   14. bookmark
15. RAM   16. e-mail   17. laptop   18. mouse   19. byte   20. password   21. server
22. browser   23. bug   24. CPU   25. software   26. chip   27. download   28. homepage
29. search engine   30. CD-ROM

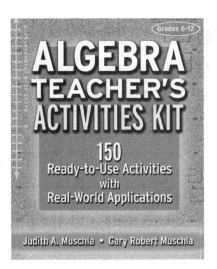

Algebra Teacher's Activities Kit:
150 Ready-to-Use Activities with Real-World Applications

Paper / 352 pages
ISBN: 0-7879-6598-7

Get creative and challenging algebra activities—that require minimal teacher preparation—at your fingertips with the *Algebra Teacher's Activities Kit.* This unique math resource contains 150 fun and imaginative ideas, in ten sections, that follow a pre-algebra and algebra curriculum and support NCTM standards.

Developed to motivate and challenge students, these exercises focus on real-life applications and cover all key topics. They can be used as a supplement to reinforce skills and concepts previously taught, for extra credit assignments, or to assist substitute teachers.

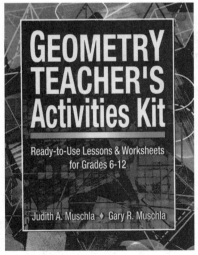

Geometry Teacher's Activities Kit:
Ready-to-Use Lessons & Worksheets for Grades 6-12

Paper / 384 pages
ISBN: 0-13-060038-5

This unique resource provides 130 detailed lessons with reproducible worksheets to help students understand geometry concepts and recognize and interpret geometry's relationship to the real world. The lessons and worksheets are organized into seven sections, each covering one major area of geometry and presented in a consistent and easy-to-follow format, including a learning objective, special materials (if any), teaching notes with step-by-step directions, answer key, and reproducible student activity sheets. Activities in sections 1–6 are presented in order of difficulty within each section while those in Section 7, "A Potpourri of Geometry," are open-ended and may be used with most middle and high school classes. Many activities throughout the book may be used with calculators and computers in line with the NCTM's recommendations.

Math Starters!
5- to 10-Minute Activities That Make Kids Think, Grades 6-12

Paper / 336 pages
ISBN: 0-87628-566-3

Here is a super collection of over 650 ready-to-use math starters that get kids quickly focused and working on math as soon as they enter your classroom! Perfect for any math curriculum, these high-interest problems spark involvement in the day's lesson, help students build necessary skills, and allow you to handle daily management tasks without wasting valuable instructional time. For easy use, all of the math-starter problems are printed in a big 8½" x 11" format that folds flat for photocopying, and they are organized into two parts. Part I, "Making Math Starters a Part of Your Program," gives you practical suggestions for implementing math starters in your teaching routine, and Part II, "Math Starters," provides collections of math-starter problems related to six major areas of secondary math, including: Whole Numbers; Theory & Operations; Fractions, Decimals & Percents; Measurement; Geometry; Algebra; and Potpourri.

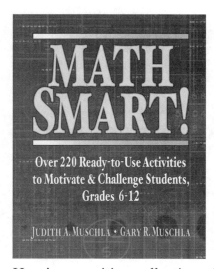

Math Smart!
Over 220 Ready-to-Use Activities to Motivate & Challenge Students, Grades 6-12

Paper / 400 pages
ISBN: 0-7879-6642-8

Here's an exciting collection of 222 reproducible activity sheets to stimulate and challenge your students in all areas of math—from whole numbers to data analysis—while emphasizing problem solving, critical thinking, and the use of technology for today's curriculum!

These activities teach students how to think with numbers, recognize relationships, and make connections between mathematical concepts. You pick the activity appropriate for their needs . . . let them self-check their answers . . . encourage the use of a calculator . . . or provide further challenges with activities that have multiple answers.

For quick and easy use, all of these ready-to-use activities are organized into seven convenient sections and printed in a lay-flat format for easy photocopying of any page as many times as needed.

Hands-On Math Projects With Real-Life Applications:

Ready-to-Use Lessons and Materials for Grades 6-12

Paper / 384 pages
ISBN: 0-13-032015-3

A collection of 60 hands-on investigations to help students apply math concepts and skills to everyday problems found across the curriculum, in sports, and in daily life. These tested projects stress cooperative learning, group sharing, and writing, and then build skills in problem-solving, critical thinking, decision-making, and computation. Each project follows the same proven format, including instructions for the teacher, a Student Guide, and one or more reproducible datasheets and worksheets. To help find appropriate projects quickly, a special Skills Index identifies the skills emphasized in each project, and all materials are organized into 6 major sections: Math & Science ~ Math & Social Studies ~ Math & Language ~ Math & Art & Music ~ Math & Sports & Recreation ~ Math & Life Skills.

Available Spring 2005:

The Math Teacher's Book of Lists, 2nd Edition

Paper / 250 pages (est.)
ISBN: 0-7879-7398-X

Hands-On Algebra!
Ready-to-Use Games & Activities for Grades 7-12

Frances M. Thompson

Paper / 640 pages
ISBN: 0-87628-386-5

Lay a solid foundation of algebra proficiency with over 155 hands-on games and activities. Through a unique three-step approach, students gain mastery over algebra concepts and skills one activity at a time, helping learners to seek patterns and retain and test what they have learned. These materials encourage exploration and the application of newly learned concepts and skills.

Algebra Out Loud:
Learning Mathematics Through Reading and Writing Activities

Pat Mower, Ph.D.

Paper / 256 pages
ISBN: 0-7879-6898-6

You probably know that some of the best "teachable" moments occur when the classroom is abuzz with students talking to each other about math. But how do you harness that energy and turn it into effective teaching? With *Algebra Out Loud* you'll focus on fostering and promoting "math talk" in your classrooms as students learn to express their mathematical thinking.

190 Ready-to-Use Activities That Make Math Fun!

George Watson; illustrated by Alan Anthony

Paper / 364 pages
ISBN: 0-7879-6585-5

Here are 190 high-interest, ready-to-use activities to help students master basic math skills, including whole numbers, decimals, fractions, percentages, money concepts, geometry and measurement, charts and graphs, and pre-algebra for use with students of varying ability levels. All the activities are classroom-tested and presented in a variety of entertaining formats, such as puzzles, crosswords, matching, word/number searches, number substitutions, and more.